Growing Up with God: Teacher's Guide

Ordering Information: Special discounts are available on quantity purchases by corporations, associations, and others. For details, contact Info@bolzministries.com.

All Scripture quotations, unless otherwise indicated, are taken from The Message. Copyright © 1993, 1994, 1995, 1996, 2000, 2001, 2002. Used by permission of NavPress Publishing Group.

Scriptures marked NIV are take from The Holy Bible, New International Version®, NIV®. Copyright ©1973, 1978, 1984, 2011 by Biblica, Inc.™ Used by permission of Zondervan. All rights reserved worldwide. www.zondervan.com The "NIV" and "New International Version" are trademarks registered in the United States Patent and Trademark Office by Biblica, Inc.™

Cover design by Yvonne Parks www.pearcreative.ca
Editing by Inksnatcher
Book Layout by Odia Reimer www.odiareimer.com
Growing Up with God: Teacher's Guide/Shawn Bolz. —first ed.
ISBN 978-1-942306-74-0

SHAWN BOLZ

TABLE OF CONTENTS

INTRODUCTION FROM THE AUTHOR   VI

FOR PARENTS   VII

SUGGESTED USE OF THIS BOOK   VIII

TIME ALLOCATION   X

CHAPTER 1   1

Teaching Point 1: Connect with God as a friend.
Teaching Point 2: Friendship with God is interactive.
Teaching Point 3: You can learn how to listen to God.

CHAPTER 2   23

Teaching Point 4: Go on a journey with your close friends and family.
Teaching Point 5: Treasure what God tells you.
Teaching Point 6: Help others have faith to connect to God.

CHAPTER 3   46

Teaching Point 7: God has a bigger picture in mind when He tells you things.
Teaching Point 8: Your process is sometimes different from everyone else's.
Teaching Point 9: God can show you what is possible through others.

CHAPTER 4   67

Teaching Point 10: Recognize the presence of God and take chances.
Teaching Point 11: Take small steps of risk to start growing.
Teaching Point 12: Be on the lookout for ways to apply words to current circumstances.

CHAPTER 5   89

Teaching Point 13: Sometimes God leads you to your goals in indirect ways.
Teaching Point 14: Sometimes life has obstacles in the way of your promises.
Teaching Point 15: You are always called to the who, not the what.

CHAPTER 6   111

Teaching Point 16: Listen to God, even when what He tells you to do is hard.
Teaching Point 17: See what he is doing in and through your life.
Teaching Point 18: God is always teaching you and sharing Himself with you.

CHAPTER 7   133

Teaching Point 19: Your goal is to love.
Teaching Point 20: Take risks with what you hear from God.
Teaching Point 21: When you obey God and walk with Him, you can't help but
                   feel His friendship.

CHAPTER 8   155

Teaching Point 22: Your friendship with God even helps those who don't know Him!
Teaching Point 23: You can bless others by giving away what God has given you.
Teaching Point 24: God brings something good out of everything.

CHAPTER 9   177

Teaching Point 25: God speaks out of relationship and grows your relationship with Him.
Teaching Point 26: When God isn't speaking, it is because He wants you to grow
                   in your identity.
Teaching Point 27: When you act like Jesus with your friends, there is always a benefit.

CHAPTER 10   199

Teaching Point 28: You can love well.
Teaching Point 29: The number-one way people become Christians is through relationship.
Teaching Point 30: You grow in God every day.

GLOSSARY   199

TEACHERS REPRODUCIBLE PAGES   241

INTRODUCTION FROM THE AUTHOR

We wanted to write a guide that could help you teach our wonderful *Growing Up with God* book and Workbook in whatever setting that suits you. We have broken it up in several different ways to make it easy to use as a Sunday School leader, a homeschool family, or even to lead a small group at your house. We also have so many activities, lessons, and questions that you can teach a thirty-week class on this if you choose to. Whether you need the DVDs to carry the teaching or you want to do that part yourself, we've supplemented it with your choice of activations or activity pages. We've tried to give you lots of options because we passionately care about the material in hand.

I was raised in a Christian home, and my parents are my spiritual parents, as well as some of my heroes. They had to lean into the Holy Spirit so much when I was growing up, and they modeled not only strength, but also process. We wanted to give teachers, parents, and friends language and tools to help children press into their relational process with God and help them form the identity of hearing God's voice for themselves.

Our adult version of this book is called *Translating God: Hearing God's Voice for Yourself and The World Around You*, but when we were writing the kids' version, we realized they would need a two-step process. We needed to write a book and curriculum for kids to help them really gain identity through their relationship with God first, not prophecy and the gifts of the Spirit. We realized this would mean creating a two-part curriculum. This one is about children hearing God's voice for themselves, and also building the character and nature needed to mature in their relationship with God. We will release a curriculum in the future that will be about hearing God for the world around them, and that one will teach kids to prophesy, get words of knowledge, evangelize, and more. Both are important steps, but we wanted to start out with foundation.

You'll find that most of the Bible verses I quote in the Workbook and in this Teacher's Guide are from The Message Bible. I favor The Message over other translations in the *Growing Up with God* study course because it's so easy for children to understand, and it's a step up from a children's Bible version, which is prone to miss out key parts of Scripture and focuses more on stories.

Thank you so much for getting this tool! Please send us feedback and testimonies of what worked, and feel free to tell us what we can do better in the future as well. This was a new type of project for us, and we want to grow in our ability to help you!

Shawn Bolz
Author

FOR PARENTS

We wanted to add a component to these materials that would give you tips on how to disciple and be spiritual parents as well as natural parents to your kids. As older Christians, we often get the question: "Who is your spiritual father or mother?" We trust parents are both, and we believe in you and your role of mentoring your children in their spiritual journey right now!

As a matter of fact, I came from a family where my spiritual parents are my natural parents. They did many important things to keep me connected to them and to God. We are believing the same for our children—that they will look to us in our role as their spiritual parents as well as their natural ones. I've written some notes for parents throughout the curriculum, because parents who use these materials have even more of a voice and consistency than a Sunday school leader, small group leader, or a pastor would.

If your job is to grow your child up in God, then God has given you the grace, the tools, and the right mix of love and relationship for the job at hand! Maybe you already do some of the things we suggest in this Teacher's Guide, so we are just reinforcing their importance, or maybe our suggestions will present you with a new way of thinking.

Ultimately we wanted parents to also be able to use this study course as a tool to disciple their children with. Whether you are a homeschool family already and used to teaching your children with materials like these, or if you are a parent needing a tool to help strengthen your children's spiritual lives, we believe God will use you powerfully to help your children understand what He is telling them. We hope these tips are useful to you.

SUGGESTED USE OF THIS BOOK

Each chapter of this Teacher's Guide will include the components mentioned below.

 Chapter Overview/Checklist – The structural breakdown of all of the components in the Teacher's Guide. This will be the teacher's "guide" and checklist to the flow and core components in the chapter.

 Teaching Points Overview – A three-bullet overview of the Teaching Points in the chapter.

 DVD Session – Each chapter is also accompanied with a correlating DVD session. For example, DVD session 1 goes with Chapter 1 in the Teacher's Guide. The DVDs are composed of a few components.

1. The story synopsis for the relating chapter from *Growing Up with God*
2. A life story from Shawn that relates to topics in the chapter
3. Lesson overview of topics that the session will cover
4. Lesson 1
5. Lesson 2
6. Lesson 3
7. Growth prayer

 Child's Testimony – A testimony from a child who has been taught the principles of growing up with God.

 Chapter Synopsis – A topical summary of the correlating chapter in *Growing Up with God*.

 Biblical Foundations – A supporting paragraph and Scripture to assist the teacher in presenting the topics in the Teacher's Guide. Each Biblical Foundations entry includes an inspiring breakdown of a Scripture and scriptural reference. Biblical Foundations entries allow the teacher to go deeper in a subject, adding even more to the DVD session and primary teaching text. They can be used for a backdrop of understanding or they can be taught straight out of the book. As you prepare, inspire, and teach, the Biblical Foundation entries will help you to be rooted and grounded in the Word.

 Student Key Verse – A verse highlighted in the primary teaching text. It is good to identify the Key Verse as you share from the story.

Teaching Content – This is the primary teaching content for the Teacher's Guide. All of the teaching sections come from the Workbook and were built around *Growing Up with God*. The *Growing Up with God* Workbook will also include the Teaching Points that are in the Teacher's Guide. The content is centered around a discipleship journey of connecting with God first—for yourself and for those around you. Your children's relationships and their life journeys are a core focus throughout the *Growing Up with God* content. We have included all thirty teachings from the Workbook in the Teacher's Guide.

 Student Question/Reflection – The Student Question/Reflection time is a direct application of the topics presented in each Teaching Point and chapter, designed to allow the teacher and student to apply the concepts and stories to their practical lives. Students will be strengthened, challenged, and helped to grow in healthy ways in this section.

 Tips for Parents: In some, but not all, of the teaching content, we have included tips for parents on how to practically integrate the Teaching Points into a child's life and into family life.

 Growth Prayer – Growth Prayers are engaging prayers that close out the chapter with an invitation for God to strengthen, impart, support, encourage, and teach children more about him. All of the Growth Prayers relate to the topics that are presented in the lesson plan.

 Individual Activity – The *Growing Up with God* Workbook can be completed independently. The Workbook features an Individual Activity for each chapter. Activities will vary chapter by chapter.

 Group Activity- The *Growing Up with God* Workbook can also be completed in a group setting. The Workbook features a group exercise for each chapter. Activities will vary chapter by chapter. Some typical classroom supplies may be needed.

 Activation Page - The *Growing Up with God* Teacher's Guide has included an Activation page at the end of each chapter with the correlating instructions. The activation pages can only be found in the Teacher's Guide. All Activation pages will also be included in the back of the Teacher's Guide on a perforated page, which can be removed and copied for duplication. Activities will vary chapter by chapter. Some typical classroom supplies may be needed.

 Coloring Page – Coloring pages are included in each chapter as a bonus activity for your individual or group setting. All Coloring Pages are included at the end of each chapter. A perforated page is also included at the end of the Teacher's Guide for copying purposes.

TIME ALLOCATION

The *Growing Up with God* Teacher's Guide has a lot to offer. We have included many components from *Growing Up with God*, as well as the Workbook, Coloring Book, and DVD sessions. We know the individual and group use of the Teacher's Guide components may vary in time and application from group to group. Nevertheless, we have put together a simplified, estimated timeframe for each Teacher's Guide component, along with three proposed plans.

10 WEEK LITE PLAN

- Complete one chapter in the Teacher's Guide each week.
- Read one chapter in *Growing Up with God* at a separate time.
- Watch one DVD session per week.
- Complete group and activity components in each chapter of the Workbook. Individual activations can be completed at a separate time.
- Estimated time of completion is between 50 minutes for each chapter, depending on the speed of class and class participation.

10 WEEK FULL PLAN

- Complete one chapter in the Teacher's Guide each week.
- Read one chapter in *Growing Up with God*.
- Watch one DVD session per week.
- Complete all components in each chapter of the Workbook.
- Estimated time of completion is between 115–135 minutes for each chapter, depending on the speed of class and class participation.

30 WEEK PLAN

- Complete one Teaching Point each week for thirty weeks.
- Each DVD contains three Teaching Points. Just play one at a time.
- Divide reading *Growing Up with God* between 30 weeks, or assign the reading outside of the class setting.
- Assign one activation per week between the individual, group, activity pages, or coloring pages.
- Estimated time of completion is between 35–45 minutes for each session, depending on speed of the class and class participation.

ESTIMATED TIME OF EACH COMPONENT:

- **Read a chapter in *Growing up with God* in class:** 10-15 minutes
- **Read Story Synopsis:** 1-3 minutes
- **Watch DVD:** 10 minutes (average time)
- **Read/Review Teaching Content:** 7-10 minutes
- **Student Question/Reflection time:** 10 minutes
- **Class participation and review of Question/Reflection time:** 10 - 15 minutes
- **Individual Growth Activity:** 10 minutes
- **Group Growth Activity:** 10 minutes
- **Student Activation:** 10 minutes
- **Coloring Page:** 15 - 30 minutes

OPTIONS FOR SHOWING DVD SESSIONS

OPTION 1:

Watch entire Session and go back and review all three Teaching Points together.

Growth Prayer - Pray with Shawn on the DVD.

OPTION 2:

1. Watch the Chapter synopsis, Shawn's engaging story, and Teaching Point 1.
2. Pause the DVD for Student Question/Reflection activity.
3. Resume DVD for Teaching Point 2.
4. Pause the DVD for Student Question/Reflection activity.
5. Resume DVD for Teaching Point 3.
6. Pause the DVD for Student Question/Reflection activity.

Growth Prayer - Pray with Shawn on the DVD.

CHAPTER 1 CHECKLIST

☐ Read Chapter 1 in *Growing Up with God*
☐ Choose DVD – Option One or Two
☐ Read aloud: Student testimonials
☐ Review with Students: Synopsis

TEACHING POINT 1:
CONNECTING WITH GOD AS A FRIEND

☐ Teach / Review Biblical Foundations
Biblical Foundations 1.1:
"Believing Births Friendship"
☐ Share: Student Key Verse
John 10:10
☐ Teach / Review: Teaching Content 1
Connecting with God as a Friend
☐ Student Question / Reflection
When was the first time you felt like God was your friend? What did you feel? Maybe you didn't feel anything but you just knew. How did you know?

TEACHING POINT 2:
HOW FRIENDSHIP WITH GOD IS INTERACTIVE

☐ Teach / Review Biblical Foundations
Biblical Foundations 1.2:
"God Covers Us with Friendship"
☐ Share: Student Key Verse
John 16:7
☐ Teach / Review: Teaching Content 2
How Friendship is Interactive
☐ Student Question / Reflection
The Holy Spirit was Jesus's friend, and they had a lot of fun and good conversations together. Jesus said the Holy Spirit takes from God and delivers it to you. What do you think of that?

TEACHING POINT 3:
LEARN HOW TO LISTEN

☐ Teach / Review Biblical Foundation
Biblical Foundations 1.3:
"Practice Listening"
☐ Share: Student Key Verse
John 10:3
☐ Teach / Review: Teaching Content 3
Learning How to Listen
☐ Student Question / Reflection
Maria was worried that she might never be able to hear God talk to her. Have you ever worried about that too, and have you talked to God about it? He can always hear you. Write down anything you're nervous about when you think about hearing God talk to you.

PRAY GROWTH PRAYER

GROWTH ACTIVITIES

☐ Individual
☐ Group
☐ Activity Page
☐ Coloring Page
☐ Implement parenting tip into weekly life

Growing Up with God

CHAPTER 1

TEACHER GUIDE - CHAPTER 1 OVERVIEW

CHAPTER 1 OVERVIEW

☐ Teaching Overview ☐ DVD Session 1
☐ Chapter Synopsis ☐ Growth Prayer

TEACHING POINT 1:
CONNECTING WITH GOD AS A FRIEND

1. Biblical Foundations 1.1:
"Believing Births Friendship"
2. Student Key Verse: John 10:10
3. Teaching Content 1
4. Student Question: *When was the first time you felt like God was your friend? What did you feel? Maybe you didn't feel anything but you just knew. How did you know?*

TEACHING POINT 3:
LEARNING HOW TO LISTEN

1. Biblical Foundations 1.3:
"Practice Listening"
2. Student Key Verse: John 10:3
3. Teaching Content 3
4. Student Question: *Maria was worried that she might never be able to hear God talk to her. Have you ever worried about that too, and have you talked to God about it? He can always hear you. Write down anything you're nervous about when you think about hearing God talk to you.*

TEACHING POINT 2:
FRIENDSHIP WITH GOD IS INTERACTIVE

1. Biblical Foundations 1.2:
"God Covers Us with Friendship"
2. Student Key Verse: John 16:7
3. Teaching Content 2
4. Student Question: *The Holy Spirit was Jesus' friend, and they had a lot of fun and good conversations together. Jesus said the Holy Spirit takes from God and delivers it to you. What do you think of that?*

GROWTH ACTIVITIES

1. Individual
2. Group
3. Activity Page
4. Coloring Page
5. Growth Prayer

STORY SYNOPSIS

Maria, Lucas, and Harper are at summer camp, where they've been learning about friendship with God. Maria is starting to get to know God better. Harper and Lucas are her best friends, and they are a little further along.

On the last night of the camp, their group activity is to pray with each other to hear the voice of God. Even though Maria loves summer camp, she is nervous and stressed out about this part of it because she has never really heard God's voice and is afraid she might never be able to hear Him speak to her. Lucas and Harper encourage Maria to listen to God. When she does hear something, they help her figure out what to do next. They all hear different things that encourage them on their God-journey.

CHILD'S TESTIMONY

Lucy's Testimony, Age 9

I asked one of my leaders, Rey, if he was sick or in pain. "No, but you can give me a prophetic word," he replied. My mom reminded me of what I had learned about hearing from God, so I listened and then looked up at him and said, "I see God advancing your career soon." Rey began to laugh and explained he had been up for a promotion for several months and it kept getting delayed. He worked with one of the very big companies in town. The very next week, he told us that he got the promotion!

LET'S GET STARTED

Let's jump right into Chapter one! If you have elected to have your students read each chapter as they go along with the DVDs, then now is the time to read Chapter one in *Growing Up with God*. If your students are reading their book outside of your class setting, then please skip down to the teaching points.

PLAY DVD SESSION 1

OPTION 1:

Watch the entire session one and go back and review all three teaching points together.

OPTION 2:

1. Watch the Chapter one synopsis, Shawn's engaging story, and Teaching Point one.
2. Pause the DVD for Student Question/ Reflection activity.
3. Resume DVD for Teaching Point two.
4. Pause the DVD for Student Question/ Reflection activity.
5. Resume DVD for Teaching Point three.
6. Pause the DVD for Student Question/ Reflection activity.

GROWTH PRAYER
PRAY ALONG WITH SHAWN ON THE DVD GROWTH PRAYER

Say this out loud: God, thank You for being a real friend to me even when I don't see it. And I choose to be Your real friend. Help me to interact with you in real ways, like friends do. Would You show me how You talk to me and teach me how to listen to Your voice? Thank You.

Amen!

Now you have taken a big step in growing up with God!

Did you know the *Growing Up with God* **Workbooks** have a built in Students Notes section?

Encourage your Students to write down some notes during the DVD's.

Teacher Notes:

_____

_____

_____

_____

_____

_____

_____

_____

Teaching Point 1
CONNECT WITH GOD AS A FRIEND

Page 4

CONNECT WITH GOD AS A FRIEND

TEACHING POINT 1

1. Biblical Foundations 1.1:
"Believing Births Friendship"
2. Student Key Verse: John 10:10
3. Teaching Content 1
4. Student Question: *When was the first time you felt like God was your friend? What did you feel? Maybe you didn't feel anything but you just knew. How did you know?*

1.1 BIBLICAL FOUNDATIONS: BELIEVING BIRTHS FRIENDSHIP

There are many people in the Scriptures who we can look to and say that they were friends of God. Abraham is one of the most memorable people in the Bible. His name actually means "God's friend" (James 2:23). Abraham believed and trusted God throughout his life, even though he had many difficulties and obstacles. His love for God actually created faith for impossible things to happen for him, and God loved that! God loves to see His purposes and good intentions being believed in, just like we like it when people know and believe in us. This kind of belief is called faith, and God said that because Abraham had faith, he was His friend.

"'Abraham believed God and was set right with God,' includes his action. It's that mesh of believing and acting that got Abraham named God's friend." — James 2:23 MSG

Student Key Verse

John 10:10: "I came so they can have real and eternal life, more and better life than they ever dreamed of."

CONNECT WITH GOD AS A FRIEND

Did you know that God made you for friendship? God made people because He wanted to share everything He had made with them. He wanted us! He wanted friends, companions, and kids like you who He could be with all the time. We can know Him and also connect to Him! Just like a computer connects to Wi-Fi, you are connected by your spirit to the heart of God. His heart is massive, His love reaches everywhere, and it can help you live the best kind of life.

Paul said, "God can do anything, you know—far more than you could ever imagine or guess or request in your wildest dreams! He does it not by pushing us around but by working within us, his Spirit deeply and gently within us" (Ephesians 3:20). That is friendship language! God gives us His Spirit to help us connect to Him as a friend. He works deeply within us! Jesus knew that kids would understand this. You are not less important than grownups in the kingdom of God! He is ready to invest real time with you now!

God was thinking about you for millions of years before He ever created you. It's just like an artist who thinks about what he's going to paint for ages before he starts to paint his best creation! God spent time thinking of what you would like, what would make you happy, what kind of personality you would have, and what kinds of dreams you would dream. Thinking about spending forever with you made Him really happy.

Jesus says, "I came so they can have real and eternal life, more and better life than they ever dreamed of" (John 10:10). He said this about you! He made you. He created you to have a quality of friendship with Him that is epic. He created you to have a quality of eternal life that will be awesome—even here on earth! He made you to connect with Him as a friend both on earth and in heaven.

Teacher Notes

_____

_____

_____

_____

_____

_____

_____

_____

_____

_____

_____

_____

_____

_____

_____

_____

_____

Student
Question/Reflection

When was the first time you felt like God was your friend? What did you feel? Maybe you didn't feel anything but you just knew. How did you know?

_____

_____

_____

_____

_____

_____

_____

QUESTION/REFLECTION

Question/Reflection

When was the first time you felt like God was your
friend? What did you feel? Maybe you didn't feel
anything but you just knew. How did you know?

WORKBOOK CHAPTER 1 7

_____

_____

_____

_____

_____

_____

_____

_____

_____

Teaching Point 2

FRIENDSHIP WITH GOD IS INTERACTIVE

FRIENDSHIP WITH GOD IS INTERACTIVE

TEACHING POINT 2

1. Biblical Foundations 1.2:
"God Covers Us with Friendship"
2. Student Key Verse: John 16:7
3. Teaching Content 2
4. Student Question: *The Holy Spirit was Jesus' friend, and they had a lot of fun and good conversations together. Jesus said the Holy Spirit takes from God and delivers it to you. What do you think of that?*

1.2 BIBLICAL FOUNDATIONS:
GOD COVERS US WITH FRIENDSHIP

Job (from the Bible) was thinking back to his earlier years in life, and he talked about how God's friendship graced his home. Another version of the Bible says God's friendship covered Job with intimate fellowship. Job was connected to God in a deep, personal way, and he called it real friendship. Because of this, he benefitted from knowing God's secrets and His counsel, and he had His trust. We, too, can be in this friendship with God. He desires to cover our home with friendship. The home is our place of safety, intimacy, rest, life, and it's our center of love.

"Oh, how I miss those golden years when God's friendship graced my home." – Job 29:4

Student Key Verse

John 16:7: "If I don't leave, the Friend won't come.
But if I go, I'll send him to you."

Teacher Notes

FRIENDSHIP WITH GOD IS INTERACTIVE

Friendship with God is interactive, which means that you always get to share and talk with God about everything. The Bible shows us that God spent great time and energy connecting to those He loved as a good friend.

Friendships get better with friends you care about and talk to a lot. You can grow into this friendship with God and grow up with God. Jesus was always talking to God. He even said that because of the Holy Spirit in you, you would have the same kind of relationship with God He has. That means you will hear what the Father is saying to you too!

Jesus even explained this to the disciples and called the Holy Spirit "the Friend." "If I don't leave, the Friend won't come. But if I go, I'll send him to you. I still have many things to tell you, but you can't handle them now. But when the Friend comes, the Spirit of the Truth, he will take you by the hand and guide you into all the truth there is. He won't draw attention to himself, but will make sense out of what is about to happen and, indeed, out of all that I have done and said. He will honor me; he will take from me and deliver it to you. Everything the Father has is also mine. That is why I've said, 'He takes from me and delivers to you'" (John 16:7, 12-15).

Jesus spent time with God like He was a real friend, not just a person way out there or far away. What did this friendship look like? Spending time together, sharing ideas with God, having fun with God. This friendship showed loyalty—sticking up for God's heart, trusting God to care for His safety and well-being, and working on the skills to keep His friendship going. When you're friends with God, you get to do stuff with Him.

Student Question/Reflection

The Holy Spirit was Jesus' friend, and they had a lot of fun and good conversations together. Jesus said the Holy Spirit takes from God and delivers it to you. What do you think of that?

QUESTION/REFLECTION

Question/Reflection

The Holy Spirit was Jesus's friend, and they had a lot of fun and good conversations together. Jesus said the Holy Spirit takes from God and delivers it to you. What do you think of that?

WORKBOOK CHAPTER 1

💡 TIP FOR PARENTS:

Connecting to your child/children by relating personal experience while engaging theirs is key. Try it here: Talk about the best friend you have ever had and engage your child in a conversation about what friendship is. Pick someone other than your spouse, just so they can relate a little more (sometimes when it is just you as parents, they can't imagine or relate to your story). Ask them about their closest friendships and what kinds of things make them close friends. Share about a friend who you don't keep connected to and why. Then share about one you do keep connected to, and why it has worked so well. Use this time to get to know what their friendships are like when doors are closed or when they are alone together. What are they enjoying? What makes the friendships special? Ask them if there are any areas they like about their friendships that they would want to have with God as well.

Teaching Point 3

YOU CAN LEARN HOW TO LISTEN TO GOD

YOU CAN LEARN HOW TO LISTEN TO GOD

TEACHING POINT 3

1. Biblical Foundations 3:
"Practice Listening"
2. Student Key Verse: John 10:3
3. Teaching Content 3
4. Student Question: *Maria was worried that she might never be able to hear God talk to her. Have you ever worried about that too, and have you talked to God about it? He can always hear you. Write down anything you're nervous about when you think about hearing God talk to you.*

1.3 BIBLICAL FOUNDATIONS: PRACTICE LISTENING

Samuel (in the Bible) was new to listening to God and needed some practice. It was nighttime when God spoke to Samuel the first time. "Then God called out, 'Samuel, Samuel!' Samuel answered, 'Yes? I'm here.' Then he ran to Eli saying, 'I heard you call. Here I am'" (1 Samuel 3:4-5).

Samuel thought it was his mentor, Eli, speaking to him, so he ran over and woke him up in the middle of the night. But it wasn't Eli speaking; it was God talking to Samuel. Samuel woke Eli up two more times, thinking that Eli was talking to him. Finally, "Eli directed Samuel, 'Go back and lie down. If the voice calls again, say, "Speak, God. I'm your servant, ready to listen."' Samuel returned to his bed. Then God came and stood before him exactly as before, calling out, 'Samuel! Samuel!' Samuel answered, 'Speak. I'm your servant, ready to listen'" (1 Samuel 3:9-10).

The third time God spoke to Samuel, he knew it was God. Samuel said, "Speak. I'm your servant, ready to listen." Learning to listen and then beginning to apply understanding is important! Practice makes perfect. Let's all continue to practice hearing God's voice.

Student Key Verse

John 10:3: The gatekeeper opens the gate to him and the sheep recognize his voice. He calls his own sheep by name and leads them out.

YOU CAN LEARN HOW TO LISTEN TO GOD

Teacher Notes

Jesus knew how to listen to God and so did the disciples. As a matter of fact, Jesus made it easy to understand that we all naturally hear God's voice. You were wired for it! He says that the Good Shepherd's sheep hear His voice, meaning you can hear His voice.

It takes practice to learn how to hear God in your spirit or heart. It can be hard because you are expecting to hear God talk to you in the same way you hear everyone else do it. Sometimes God's voice is like the voice in your own head. Sometimes His voice is like having a brilliant idea, and sometimes it's like a beautiful picture in your head that means something to you. When you are growing up in your friendship with God, you get to learn how He talks to you!

Maria didn't think God would talk to her. Once she was thinking about how good it felt to sing to God about her love for Him, and she saw a gentle father's face smiling and heard, "I have made you to be creative like me. You are an actress." She heard God while she was thinking about how good God was. It surprised her and she didn't even know she could pray with Jesus to hear more. She was just excited to have heard anything! She learned how to hear God by paying attention to her thoughts and pictures in her mind.

Student
Question/Reflection

Maria was worried that she might never be able to hear God talk to her. Have you ever worried about that, too, and have you talked to God about it? He can always hear you. Write down anything you're nervous about when you think about hearing God talk to you.

_____

_____

_____

_____

_____

_____

QUESTION/REFLECTION

Question/Reflection

Maria was worried that she might never be able to hear God talk to her. Have you ever worried about that too, and have you talked to God about it? He can always hear you. Write down anything you're nervous about when you think about hearing God talk to you.

WORKBOOK CHAPTER 1 · 15

_____

_____

_____

_____

_____

_____

_____

ACTIVATION

INDIVIDUAL ACTIVITY
AND INSTRUCTION

Write down three things that you think you could do more often to grow in your friendship with God. These can be things like, "Spend more time with God as a friend" or "Hear from God more." Now ask the Holy Spirit to show you a practical step you can take toward doing one or more of these things this week, like "Every morning while I'm getting dressed, I'll ask God to show me a picture in my mind of something about my day." Write down what you hear.

_____

_____

_____

_____

_____

_____

_____

_____

_____

_____

_____

ACTIVATION, CONTINUED...

GROUP ACTIVITY AND INSTRUCTION

Take turns sharing something that makes your friendship with God seem real and strong. What is the best thing about your friendship with God? Each person will then pray that blessing over everyone else in the group. For example: "The best thing about my friendship with God is when a bird flies by me when I'm in my backyard. It's like He's sending me a gift and reminding me that He knows I love nature. I pray over all of you that same blessing of being able to see God's messages in nature."

_____

_____

_____

_____

_____

_____

_____

_____

_____

_____

_____

_____

_____

GROWTH PRAYER

Say this out loud:

God, thank You for being a real friend to me, even when I don't see it. And I choose to be Your real friend.

Help me to interact with You in real ways, like friends do.

Would You show me how You talk to me and teach me how to listen to Your voice?

Thank You.

Amen!

Now you have taken a big step in growing up with God!

ACTIVATION PAGE
WHAT ATTRIBUTES ARE IMPORTANT TO ME IN FRIENDSHIP?

Write down the qualities you would want a friend of yours to have. For example: loyalty, confidentiality, bravery, fun to be around, musical talent, spiritual strength, cleverness, athleticism, relational skills, leadership qualities, celebratory personality, truthfulness, kindness, sensitivity, or helpfulness.

Scripture: "When the Friend comes, the Spirit of the Truth, he will take you by the hand and guide you into all the truth there is."
– John 16:12

PRINTABLE ACTIVATION PAGE AVAILABLE IN TEACHER REPRODUCIBLE PAGES - PAGE 241

CHAPTER 2 CHECKLIST

- ☐ Read Chapter 2 in *Growing Up with God*
- ☐ Choose DVD – Option One or Two
- ☐ Read aloud: Student testimonials
- ☐ Review with Students: Synopsis

TEACHING POINT 4:
GO ON A GOD JOURNEY WITH YOUR CLOSE FRIENDS AND FAMILY

- ☐ Teach / Review Biblical Foundations
  Biblical Foundations 2.1:
  "Jesus Starts the Best Journeys"
- ☐ Share: Student Key Verse
  Hebrews 10:23
- ☐ Teach / Review: Teaching Content 4
  Go on a God journey
- ☐ Student Question / Reflection
  Have you ever shared some things God tells you with friends and your family? How did they react?
  Lucas's mom was excited to hear Lucas talk about his word from God. She encouraged him and told him he was special. How can you encourage and help others to get more connected to God?

TEACHING POINT 5:
TREASURE WHAT GOD TELLS YOU

- ☐ Teach / Review Biblical Foundations
  Biblical Foundations 2.2:
  "God's Kingdom Is Like a Treasure"
- ☐ Share: Student Key Verse
  Luke 2:19
- ☐ Teach / Review: Teaching Content 5
  Treasure what God tells you
- ☐ Student Question / Reflection

TEACHING POINT 5: CONTINUED...
TREASURE WHAT GOD TELLS YOU

Do you treasure the things God has told you? Do you think about them when you are making decisions about your life? It's important to do! What are some things you could do to help you remember?

TEACHING POINT 6:
HELP OTHERS HAVE FAITH TO CONNECT TO GOD

- ☐ Teach / Review Biblical Foundations
  Biblical Foundations 2.3:
  "Be Jesus to the World"
- ☐ Share: Student Key Verse
  Hebrews 10:24
- ☐ Teach / Review: Teaching Content 6
  Help others have faith to connect to God
- ☐ Student Question / Reflection
  God made you to be creative about coming up with ways to connect with His heart. If you stop and think about that right now, what are some things you could start doing to connect to Him more?

PRAY GROWTH PRAYER

GROWTH ACTIVITIES

- ☐ Individual
- ☐ Group
- ☐ Activity Page
- ☐ Coloring Page
- ☐ Implement parenting tip into weekly life

Growing Up with God

CHAPTER 2

TEACHER GUIDE - CHAPTER 2 OVERVIEW

CHAPTER 2 OVERVIEW

☑ Teaching Overview   ☑ DVD Session 2

☑ Chapter Synopsis   ☑ Growth Prayer

TEACHING POINT 4:
GO ON A GOD JOURNEY WITH YOUR CLOSE FRIENDS

1. Biblical Foundations 2.1:
"Jesus Starts the Best Journeys"

2. Student Key Verse: Hebrews 10:23

3. Teaching Content 4

4. Student Question: *Have you ever shared some of the things God tells you with friends or your family? How did they react? Lucas' mom was excited to hear him talk about his word from God. She encouraged him and told him he was special. How can you encourage and help others to get more connected to God?*

TEACHING POINT 6:
HELP OTHERS HAVE FAITH TO CONNECT TO GOD

1. Biblical Foundations 2.3:
"Be Jesus To The World"

3. Student Key Verse: Hebrews 10:24

4. Teaching Content 6

5. Student Question: *God made you to be creative about coming up with ways to connect with His heart. If you stop and think about that right now, what are some things you could start doing to connect to Him more?*

TEACHING POINT 5:
TREASURE WHAT GOD TELLS YOU

1. Biblical Foundations 2.2:
"God's Kingdom Is Like a Treasure"

2. Student Key Verse: Luke 2:19

3. Teaching Content 5

4. Student Question: *Do you treasure the things God has told you? Do you think about them when you are making decisions about your life? It's important to do! What are some things you could do to help you remember?*

GROWTH ACTIVITIES

1. Individual
2. Group
3. Activity Page
4. Coloring Page
5. Growth Prayer

STORY SYNOPSIS

Lucas gets home from camp and shares all about what God did with his mom. He shares how Harper, Maria, and he prayed to hear God talk to them about their lives. He then tells his mom about his personal prophecy from the guest minister, and that it was all about being kind and helping others have a kind nature. His mom understands because God has helped her grow in love and compassion over the years too. She encourages him by telling him that God has already started growing him in those ways. She's happy about what has happened to him spiritually, which helps Lucas to value it all even more.

Lucas treasures the prophetic word he received, and also what God showed him personally. He thinks it all over in his heart and tells God he's ready to learn everything God wants him to learn about compassion and love.

CHILD'S TESTIMONY

Sophie's Testimony, Age 9

I saw the leader Johnny at camp, except he wasn't the age he is now; he was a young boy. I saw him waking up one morning. I could see his room and everything in his room. Bed, dresser, desk—everything you'd see in a normal room. I saw a gold straw hat sitting on the dresser, and it stood out to me. I saw him with this gold straw hat and he loved it and wore it all the time; he wouldn't go anywhere without it. I asked him if he wanted to make stuff like that. He said he used to want to be a fashion model and that was a real gold straw hat that he loved a lot. I think the Lord loved that he wanted to be a fashion model and He was bringing that up for him again.

LET'S GET STARTED

Let's jump right into Chapter 2! If you have elected to have your students read each chapter as they go along with the DVDs, then now is the time to read Chapter 2 in *Growing Up with God*. If your students are reading their book outside of your class setting, then please skip down to the teaching points.

PLAY DVD SESSION 2

OPTION 1:

Watch entire Session two and go back and review all three Teaching Points together.

OPTION 2:

1. Watch the Chapter two synopsis, Shawn's engaging story, and Teaching Point four.
2. Pause the DVD for Student Question/Reflection activity.
3. Resume DVD for Teaching Point five.
4. Pause the DVD for Student Question/Reflection activity.
5. Resume DVD for Teaching Point six.
6. Pause the DVD for Student Question/Reflection activity.

GROWTH PRAYER
PRAY ALONG WITH SHAWN ON THE DVD GROWTH PRAYER

God, help me to share my spiritual journey in real ways with my family and friends!

Help me to treasure what You tell me like Mary did! Also help me spur my friends and family on to grow with You, too!

Amen!

You just completed another lesson in Growing Up with God. It's time to grow!

Teacher Notes:

_____

_____

_____

_____

_____

_____

_____

_____

Teaching Point 4

GO ON A GOD JOURNEY WITH YOUR CLOSE FRIENDS AND FAMILY

GO ON A GOD JOURNEY WITH YOUR CLOSE FRIENDS AND FAMILY

TEACHING POINT 4

1. Biblical Foundations 2.1:
"Jesus Starts the Best Journeys"

2. Student Key Verse: Hebrews 10:23

3. Teaching Content 4

4. Student Question: *Have you ever shared some of the things God tells you with friends or your family? How did they react? Lucas' mom was excited to hear him talk about his word from God. She encouraged him and told him he was special. How can you encourage and help others to get more connected to God?*

2.1 BIBLICAL FOUNDATIONS: JESUS STARTS THE BEST JOURNEYS

The disciples went on an epic journey with God! They were going about their day doing what they knew how to do. Then one day, Jesus saw them and invited them on the journey of their lives! All of the disciples spent over three-and-a-half years together talking with God and asking Him questions together. They talked about what they understood about God and what they were challenged with. They became great friends in the journey of following Jesus. You can, too.

"Walking along the beach of Lake Galilee, Jesus saw two brothers: Simon (later called Peter) and Andrew. They were fishing, throwing their nets into the lake. It was their regular work. Jesus said to them, 'Come with me. I'll make a new kind of fisherman out of you. I'll show you how to catch men and women instead of perch and bass.' They didn't ask questions, but simply dropped their nets and followed" (Matthew 4:18-20).

"God's Spirit beckons. There are things to do and places to go!" — Romans 8:14

Student Key Verse

Hebrews 10:23: Let's keep a firm grip on the promises that keep us going. He always keeps his word.

GO ON A GOD JOURNEY WITH YOUR CLOSE FRIENDS AND FAMILY

God loves to share His heart with you. He can do this when you read the Bible or when you are just experiencing Him with your friends. Sometimes His talking to you sounds like thoughts in your heart or heart, and sometimes you can hear His voice. He is constantly nudging you to see things. He points out the people around you. He points them out so you can love them the same way He does, if you will just learn to recognize it is Him talking.

When God speaks to you, He loves it when you celebrate His words with your friends or family. Many times this is how He can tell you even more. Your friends and family will have insights, prayers, and encouragement for you so that you can learn more about what God is showing you. It's like when your parents or sports coaches help you in your sports journey. They help to celebrate when you do amazingly well, but also encourage and support you when it is tough. No athlete can become amazing without a community of coaches, friends, and family around.

Friends and family can help remind you of who you are when you're having a tough time. They can tell you when a something God tells you happens, or when someone's prophecy to you gets fulfilled, they will help celebrate it with you! We all get excited about what God did or is doing, and we worship Him and celebrate Him in each other. "Let's keep a firm grip on the promises that keep us going. He always keeps his word. Let's see how inventive we can be in encouraging love and helping out, not avoiding worshiping together as some do but spurring each other on, especially as we see the big Day approaching" (Hebrews 10:23-25).

This also happens when you share with your friends what you are reading in Scripture and you apply it together. Psalm 119:105 says, "By your words I can see where I'm going; they throw a beam of light on my dark path." This means that God's Word helps to guide you in relationships and life's decisions!

Student Question/Reflection

Have you ever shared some of the things God tells you with friends or your family?
How did they react?

Lucas's mom was excited to hear Lucas talk about his word from God. She encouraged him and told him he was special. How can you encourage and help others get more connected to God?

QUESTION/REFLECTION

Question/Reflection

Lucas's mom was excited to hear Lucas talk about his word from God, and she encouraged him and told him he was special. How can you encourage and help others get more connected to God?

WORKBOOK CHAPTER 2 27

TIP FOR PARENTS:

Parent, you are built to be a spiritual mentor for your kids! God has given you everything you need to disciple them well! One of the most important parts of going on a God-journey with your children is to listen to their God stories and celebrate them. Sometimes we are tempted to say, "That happened to me to…," and then tell a long story. While for adults, this can establish relational rapport, for kids, it can oftentimes make it seem like you don't think their stories are original or significant. Kids want to feel like what they are getting is unique, and sometimes comparison can make them feel like you don't value what God is doing with them. Let their stories stand alone and celebrate them, unless they ask if something similar has ever happened to you. Also, get in the habit of asking them what God is doing with them. Here are some helpful questions:

- ☐ Is anything in the Bible coming alive for you?
- ☐ Has God spoken anything cool to you lately?
- ☐ What is your favorite thing that God has done for you this month?
- ☐ How is your prayer life?

You won't always develop quality time around these questions, but don't worry—if you are consistent and truly interested, your kids will open up to you.

Teaching Point 5
TREASURE WHAT GOD TELLS YOU

TREASURE WHAT GOD TELLS YOU

TEACHING POINT 5

1. Biblical Foundations 2.2:
"God's Kingdom Is Like a Treasure"
2. Student Key Verse: Luke 2:19
3. Teaching Content 5
4. Student Question: *Do you treasure the things God has told you? Do you think about them when you are making decisions about your life? It's important to do! What are some things you could do to help you remember?*

2.2 BIBLICAL FOUNDATIONS: GOD'S KINGDOM IS LIKE A TREASURE.

God speaks to everyone today. He didn't always talk so much. When God speaks, His words create life. He spoke the world into existence, and now He speaks to you and to me. Wow! What a special life we have in speaking with the God who created us. We need to treasure each and every word He says. When you have real treasure in your hand, how much do you care for it? You always know where it is and don't mishandle it. Why? Because it is valuable to you. God is our treasure. Let us value Him and what He says.

"God's kingdom is like a treasure hidden in a field for years and then accidentally found by a trespasser. The finder is ecstatic—what a find!—and proceeds to sell everything he owns to raise money and buy that field." – Matthew 13:44

Student Key Verse

Luke 2:19: Mary kept all these things to herself, holding them dear, deep within herself.

TREASURE WHAT GOD TELLS YOU

God tells you things so that you can know what He is going to do in you and through you. It helps to build your confidence and your faith, and you get to see which areas you need to grow in. When the angel came and told Mary about baby Jesus and that she would be His mom, she was in awe of God's love and respect toward her. She was amazed that He picked her. She had a lot to think about! Luke says, "But Mary treasured up all these things and pondered them in her heart" (Luke 2:19).

When you ponder something in your heart, it means you're always aware of it. You always know it's there. It's carrying around what God has said to you as though it's about to happen at any moment. You don't let it leave your thoughts. You make sure God's words and promises are always a part of how you see your day and your life. That's what Lucas did. He heard the word "brotherhood." He didn't know what God was telling him about, but he pondered it and asked God about it. He knew it was a mystery that God would explain and make happen in the future, and he chose to keep his heart connected to the word.

Have you ever wanted a new toy and knew that if you asked for it for Christmas or your birthday, you would probably get it? If you knew that, then every day you would think about the enjoyment of getting that toy until it came! You can do exactly the same thing with what God tells you. You can think about it every day and smile, knowing that God loves to make His promises come true!

Teacher Notes

Student Question/Reflection

Do you treasure the things God has told you? Do you think about them when you are making decisions about your life? It's important to do! What are some things you could do to help you remember?

QUESTION/REFLECTION

Question/Reflection

Do you treasure the things God has told you? Do you think about them when you are making decisions about your life? It's important to do! What are some things you could do to help you remember?

WORKBOOK CHAPTER 2 31

_____

_____

_____

_____

_____

_____

_____

_____

TIP FOR PARENTS:

Dad or Mom, when your children hear from God, receive a prophecy from someone, or have a life-awareness moment about who they are, it is great to figure out a way to celebrate this and to keep it current in their hearts . . . because, undoubtedly, it will be challenged at some point. One of the moms I know would write sticky notes with promise Scriptures and prophetic reminders and post them to her daughter's mirror in the mornings. A dad who coaches his son's team would memorize the Scriptures that related to his son's prophetic words on the way to practice. Get creative and become a part of the process! If you model that you treasure the words they receive, it will help them to hold them with a higher value because you are their hero!

Teaching Point 6

HELP OTHERS HAVE FAITH TO CONNECT TO GOD

HELP OTHERS HAVE FAITH TO CONNECT TO GOD

TEACHING POINT 6

1. Biblical Foundations 2.3:
"Be Jesus To The World"
3. Student Key Verse: Hebrews 10:24
4. Teaching Content 6
5. Student Question: *God made you to be creative about coming up with ways to connect with His heart. If you stop and think about that right now, what are some things you could start doing to connect to Him more?*

2.3 BIBLICAL FOUNDATIONS: BE JESUS TO THE WORLD

Colossians 4:5-6 shows us the best way to help others find and grow in relationship with God: "Use your heads as you live and work among outsiders. Don't miss a trick. Make the most of every opportunity. Be gracious in your speech. The goal is to bring out the best in others in a conversation, not put them down, not cut them out." It starts off by saying, "Use your heads as you live and work among outsiders," which means you should be smart with strangers. You need to be smart to not turn your love off when you talk to them. Be kind with your words. Don't put them down with your talk or exclude them from conversations. Bring out the best in them and they are sure to find and connect with God.

Student Key Verse

Hebrews 10:24: Let's see how inventive we can be in encouraging love and helping out.

HELP OTHERS HAVE FAITH TO CONNECT TO GOD

On your spiritual journey you learn how God speaks to you. One of the amazing things that happens is that your growing connection to God helps you encourage everyone else with theirs!

We are supposed to be creative in how we can help other Christians grow in God. Remember what Paul said earlier in this chapter? "Let's see how inventive we can be in encouraging love and helping out, not avoiding worshiping together as some do but spurring each other on, especially as we see the big Day approaching" (Hebrews 10:25). God shows us how much He loves us in so many different ways each day. He's very creative about coming up with ways to help us get to know His heart better. You can be as creative as He is.

Lucas's mom was excited to hear Lucas talk about his word from God. It probably reminded her about some of the ways God had fulfilled His promises for her own life. By encouraging him, she was encouraging her own faith too.

Isn't that amazing? You get to spur others on with the love that you feel from God and the excitement you have about seeing His promises happen. Another way of looking at it is that your stories of what God does with you help to create faith in other people—they start to believe that they will have their own stories with God too. It is like receiving a power-up in a video game—you grow when you hear. In Romans 10:17, Paul says that faith comes by hearing about Jesus.

Teacher Notes

_____
_____
_____
_____
_____
_____
_____
_____
_____
_____
_____
_____
_____
_____
_____
_____
_____
_____

Student
Question/Reflection

God made you to be creative about coming up with ways to connect with His heart. If you stop and think about that right now, what are some things you could start doing to connect to Him more?

_____

_____

_____

_____

_____

_____

_____

QUESTION/REFLECTION

Question/Reflection

God made you to be creative about coming up with ways to connect with his heart. If you stop and think about that right now, what are some things you could start doing to connect to him more?

_____

_____

_____

_____

_____

_____

WORKBOOK CHAPTER 2 35

_____

_____

_____

_____

_____

_____

ACTIVATION

INDIVIDUAL ACTIVITY AND INSTRUCTION

Write a letter to God and remind Him of all the things you believe about Him, or list the things you believe He has told you you will get to do in life. Write down at least five things that you are dreaming will happen in your future, or that you feel you were made to do.

_____

_____

_____

_____

_____

_____

_____

_____

_____

_____

_____

_____

_____

_____

_____

_____

ACTIVATION, CONTINUED...

GROUP ACTIVITY AND INSTRUCTION

Practice encouragement: Sharing your dreams or the messages you feel God has given you is a vulnerable process. In this group time, have people take turns sharing something they are dreaming about doing in their lifetimes. Then the group will pray for the person sharing and encourage him or her about this dream. For example: Person 1 says, "I want to be a nurse." The group then prays or says words of encouragement over that person. "You are very nurturing! You take care of people well! I pray that God would give you understanding about how to pursue that."

_____

_____

_____

_____

_____

_____

_____

_____

_____

_____

_____

GROWTH PRAYER

God, help me to share my spiritual journey in real ways with my family and friends!

Help me to treasure what You tell me like Mary did! Also help me spur my friends and family on to grow with You too!

Amen!

You just completed another lesson in *Growing Up with God*. It's time to grow!

ACTIVATION PAGE
MY SPIRITUAL MAP MOMENTS

Write down five memories you have of moments in your life that were really important to you and God. One could be of the time when you got saved, or when you first learned how to pray. It could be a time when God spoke something to you. On the "X marks the spot" place on the map, write in the most significant of your God journey moments.

Scripture: But Mary treasured up all these things and pondered them in her heart. — Luke 2:19

PRINTABLE ACTIVATION PAGE AVAILABLE IN TEACHER REPRODUCIBLE PAGES - PAGE 241

PRINTABLE COLORING PAGE AVAILABLE IN TEACHER REPRODUCIBLE PAGES - PAGE 241

CHAPTER 3 CHECKLIST

- ☐ Read Chapter 3 in *Growing Up with God*
- ☐ Choose DVD – Option One or Two
- ☐ Read aloud: Student testimonials
- ☐ Review with Students: Synopsis

TEACHING POINT 7:
GOD HAS A BIGGER PICTURE IN MIND WHEN HE TELLS YOU THINGS

- ☐ Teach / Review Biblical Foundations
  Biblical Foundations 3.1:
  "Master Plans From God"
- ☐ Share: Student Key Verse
  Ephesians 3:20
- ☐ Teach / Review: Teaching Content 7
  God has a bigger picture
- ☐ Student Question / Reflection
  When God gives you a word or tells you something about the future, why do you think He usually make those things happen in ways you don't expect?

TEACHING POINT 8:
YOUR PROCESS IS SOMETIMES DIFFERENT EVERYONE ELSE'S

- ☐ Teach / Review Biblical Foundations
  Biblical Foundations 3.2:
  "Be Who You Are"
- ☐ Share: Student Key Verse
  Galatians 6:4-5
- ☐ Teach / Review: Teaching Content 8
  Your process is sometimes different to everyone else's
- ☐ Student Question / Reflection
  What kind of spiritual upgrades has God already given you? What has He done in your life and in your heart that has made you feel more connected to Him?

TEACHING POINT 9:
SEEING GOD MAKE THINGS HAPPEN FOR SOMEONE ELSE

- ☐ Teach / Review Biblical Foundations
  Biblical Foundations 3.3:
  "God Will Do The Same for You"
- ☐ Share: Student Key Verse
  John 14:12
- ☐ Teach / Review: Teaching Content 9
  Seeing God make things happen for someone else
- ☐ Student Question / Reflection
  What examples have you seen in your own life and in your friends' lives to prove that God wants to bless everyone with a close connection to His heart?

PRAY GROWTH PRAYER

GROWTH ACTIVITIES

- ☐ Individual
- ☐ Group
- ☐ Activity Page
- ☐ Coloring Page
- ☐ Implement parenting tip into weekly life

Growing Up with God

CHAPTER

TEACHER GUIDE - CHAPTER 3 OVERVIEW

CHAPTER 3 OVERVIEW

- ☐ Teaching Overview
- ☐ Chapter Synopsis
- ☐ DVD Session 3
- ☐ Growth Prayer

TEACHING POINT 7:
GOD HAS A BIGGER PICTURE IN MIND WHEN HE TELLS YOU THINGS

1. Biblical Foundations 3.1:
"Master Plans from God"

2. Student Key Verse: Ephesians 3:20

3. Teaching Content 7

4. Student Question: *When God gives you a word or tells you something about the future, why do you think He usually makes those things happen in ways you don't expect?*

TEACHING POINT 8:
YOUR PROCESS IS SOMETIMES DIFFERENT TO EVERYONE ELSE'S

1. Biblical Foundations 3.2:
"Be Who You Are"

2. Student Key Verse: Galatians 6:4-5

3. Teaching Content 8

4. Student Question: *What kind of spiritual upgrades has God already given you? What has He done in your life and in your heart that has made you feel more connected to Him?*

TEACHING POINT 9:
SEEING GOD MAKE THINGS HAPPEN FOR SOMEONE ELSE

1. Biblical Foundations 3.3:
"God Will Do The Same for You"

2. Student Key Verse: John 14:12

3. Teaching Content 9

4. Student Question: *What examples have you seen in your own life and in your friends' lives to prove that God wants to bless everyone with a close connection to His heart?*

GROWTH ACTIVITIES

1. Individual
2. Group
3. Activity Page
4. Coloring Page
5. Growth Prayer

STORY SYNOPSIS

Maria tries to join a drama class at the local theater because of the word about acting that she thought God gave her, but the class is full! Maria is very discouraged, because she thinks the only way the word will happen is if she takes acting classes. She wonders if she heard God at all. Harper's mom invites Maria to join the choir class at the theater with Harper, which is fun, but not the same thing to Maria.

Lucas, Harper, and Maria practice hearing God again that night, and Maria very clearly hears God give her a word for Lucas's grandmother. Harper tells Maria that if God cares that much about Lucas's grandmother having faith about selling her house, then maybe she can have faith that he's going to make her word come true too. Maria agrees and feels like her faith has grown.

CHILD'S TESTIMONY

Sarah's Testimony, Age 5

When I was around five years old and my middle brother was nearly four, we had this incredible encounter with the Holy Spirit. All of a sudden, we knew that Jesus was in the room with us and His Spirit was burning inside us. We danced like never before and then fell to the ground in praise and prayer. In those moments we both clearly heard God say (in our hearts and thoughts), "I want you two to be dance teachers in the church. My people need to know how to dance like this and enjoy Me." We were jumping on the sofas, doing cartwheels, shouting, and celebrating!

The thing is, we're both awful dancers, but God wanted us to dance with Him with all our hearts and not be afraid of what we looked like while we were doing it. Since then, we've found that it's easy for us to help draw people into God's presence. They can play with Him joyfully and be confident and alive in their worship times with Him.

LET'S GET STARTED

Let's jump right into Chapter 3! If you have elected to have your students read each chapter as they go along with the DVDs, then now is the time to read Chapter 3 in *Growing Up with God*. If your students are reading their book outside of your class setting, then please skip down to the teaching points.

PLAY DVD SESSION 3

OPTION 1:

Watch entire Session three and go back and review all three Teaching Points together.

OPTION 2:

1. Watch the Chapter three synopsis, Shawn's engaging story, and Teaching Point seven.
2. Pause the DVD for Student Question/ Reflection activity.
3. Resume DVD for Teaching Point eight.
4. Pause the DVD for Student Question/ Reflection activity.
5. Resume DVD for Teaching Point nine.
6. Pause the DVD for Student Question/ Reflection activity.

GROWTH PRAYER
PRAY ALONG WITH SHAWN ON THE DVD GROWTH PRAYER

God, I know that You always have a full picture in mind when You tell me something, and I trust You! My process may be different to everyone else's, but it is because You and I want a different result! When I see You bless someone else with heart growth or an opportunity to grow toward seeing their dream come true, help me to want and believe that You will do the same for me too.

Amen!

It's time to grow up with God!

Teacher Notes:

_____

_____

_____

_____

_____

_____

_____

_____

_____

Teaching Point 7

GOD HAS A BIGGER PICTURE IN MIND WHEN HE TELLS YOU THINGS

GOD HAS A BIGGER PICTURE IN MIND WHEN HE TELLS YOU THINGS

TEACHING POINT 7

1. Biblical Foundations 3.1:
"Master Plans from God"
2. Student Key Verse: Ephesians 3:20
3. Teaching Content 7
4. Student Question: *When God gives you a word or tells you something about the future, why do you think He usually makes those things happen in ways you don't expect?*

3.1 BIBLICAL FOUNDATIONS: MASTER PLANS FROM GOD

God's investment in his relationship with you and me is way more than we could ever comprehend. He cares so much about our life and the dreams that we have, it is amazing. God is so big, and He thinks about our lives from the beginning until the end. When God speaks, He doesn't just share information; He imparts life. Everything He says prepares us for our entire future, not just for a moment. He has a bigger picture in mind when He speaks. The picture is the best possible version of you!

"There has never been the slightest doubt in my mind that the God who started this great work in you would keep at it and bring it to a flourishing finish on the very day Christ Jesus appears."
— Philippians 1:6

Student Key Verse

Ephesians 3:20: "God can do anything, you know—far more than you could ever imagine or guess or request in your wildest dreams!"

GOD HAS A BIGGER PICTURE IN MIND WHEN HE TELLS YOU THINGS

When you start to hear from God, you will realize that what He says and what you think aren't always the same. He sometimes speaks in pictures, parables, or stories to communicate a thought to you. This is because He doesn't just want to tell you what to do. He also wants you to know His heart. Have you ever tried to tell a friend something and had to use a story or picture of what you mean to really get it across? "That was as awesome as the first time I won a prize!" This communicates how excited you are and how deeply something impacted you.

God is like this too. He doesn't just talk so you can hear what He is saying. He talks to show you what He is feeling too. When He gives you a message or a word about something he wants to do in your life, He's going to make it happen his way. He wants to do something for you that only He can do, which means you can't do it on your own or with your own abilities, even if they are good ones. You know it's Him and not you making it happen. Whenever God is doing something in you or for you, it is also for the world around you. He loves the world, and He uses your life to bring others the truth of His love.

"Take a good look, friends, at who you were when you got called into this life. I don't see many of 'the brightest and the best' among you, not many influential, not many from high-society families. Isn't it obvious that God deliberately chose men and women that the culture overlooks and exploits and abuses, chose these 'nobodies' to expose the hollow pretensions of the 'somebodies'? That makes it quite clear that none of you can get by with blowing your own horn before God" (1 Corinthians 1:26-29).

In other words, God didn't choose you because you were the best or give you great purpose because you are so skilled. He chose you knowing you couldn't be you without him! When you try something beyond your ability, just because you have faith that God wants it and will help get it done, you look like Jesus!

Teacher Notes

Student Question/Reflection

When God gives you a word or tells you something about the future, why do you think he usually make those things happen in ways you don't expect?

QUESTION/REFLECTION

Question/Reflection
When God gives you a word or tells you something about the future, why do you think he usually make those things happen in ways you don't expect?

WORKBOOK CHAPTER 3 47

_____

_____

_____

_____

_____

_____

TIP FOR PARENTS:

Many times, your kids are going to dream about things that may seem unrealistic, but popular psychology shows that parents who entertain and find enjoyment in their children's dream process actually help to build much healthier identity in their children. Sometimes our fears or practical nature of adulthood can shoot down a dream by trying to see if it's feasible before we let our children express their wonder and awe at a new idea. Practice asking your children what they want to be when they grow up, or ask them what God is showing them they are called to. Let them describe it and just enjoy them. Don't use disqualifying language like, "Well, we'll see," or "That can't become a career, but it sounds like fun." Your children aren't ready to start a career, and once they are in high school, there will be no end to the practical advice they receive. If you are comfortable with their dreams, or truly excited about what they share with you, find activities where you can invest in exploring it together. Your daughter wants to be an astronaut? Go to space camp with her. Your son wants to be an illustrator? Find some local art competitions for him to enter drawings in. By sowing into their dreaming, you will create a strong imagination, and also a "go get 'em" attitude that will stick for the real purposes they end up in. Who knows—these things they are thinking about now might be them!

Teaching Point 8

YOUR PROCESS IS SOMETIMES DIFFERENT FROM EVERYONE ELSE'S

YOUR PROCESS IS SOMETIMES DIFFERENT FROM EVERYONE ELSE'S

TEACHING POINT 8

1. Biblical Foundations 3.2:
"Be Who You Are"
2. Student Key Verse: Galatians 6:4-5
3. Teaching Content 8
4. Student Question: *What kind of spiritual upgrades has God already given you? What has He done in your life and in your heart that has made you feel more connected to Him?*

3.2 BIBLICAL FOUNDATIONS: BE WHO YOU ARE

Although we serve one God, our journeys may be different than those of our neighbors. All of Jesus's disciples were so different in their faith, their personalities, and their journeys. They each had different gifts and passions from God. God gave them confidence to feel strong and have courage with who they were. Their different paths became their unique journeys, and that is what made them special. We are all so different, and that is what God wanted.

"Let's just go ahead and be what we were made to be, without enviously or pridefully comparing ourselves with each other, or trying to be something we aren't." – Romans 12:6

Student Key Verse

Galatians 6:4-5: "Make a careful exploration of who you are and the work you have been given, and then sink yourself into that."

YOUR PROCESS IS SOMETIMES DIFFERENT FROM EVERYONE ELSE'S

You want God to work in your life and to grow your heart to be as big as His. That means you are asking for the impossible! It also means your process—the way God does that in you—isn't always the same way He does it in everyone else.

You might even be pursuing the same dreams as people who aren't saved, but you're not doing it for the same reasons they are! Many Christian kids compare themselves to their non-Christian friends and wonder why their process isn't as easy or direct. Galatians 6:4-5 says: "Make a careful exploration of who you are and the work you have been given, and then sink yourself into that. Don't be impressed with yourself. Don't compare yourself with others. Each of you must take responsibility for doing the creative best you can with your own life."

Well, you are not asking for the same results or life they are. You are asking for a spiritual and abundantly crazy, awesome life of character and good works! That means your process will be different. Jesus kept looking at the Father in heaven as His only model for how to do things. He didn't look at the people around Him. When you are walking with God, you get to learn that sometimes He won't pick a predictable way of doing things. That's because He wants you and the world around you to know that He is with you! He works in your life and causes things to happen that you couldn't do alone.

You will find that sometimes you receive an upgrade from God, much like your computer or smart device gets a new update. This happens when God shares His heart with you or when a part of the Bible comes alive in you. You have more to work with than before, even if it's only more faith.

Teacher Notes

_____

_____

_____

_____

_____

_____

_____

_____

_____

_____

_____

_____

_____

_____

_____

_____

_____

_____

Student
Question/Reflection

What kind of spiritual upgrades has God already given you? What has He done in your life and in your heart that has made you feel more connected to Him?

QUESTION/REFLECTION

Question/Reflection
What kind of spiritual upgrades has God already given you—what has he done in your life and in your heart that has made you feel more connected to him?

WORKBOOK CHAPTER 2 51

_____

_____

_____

_____

_____

_____

_____

_____

 TIP FOR PARENTS:

Helping your child understand that they are not going to be like anyone else who ever lived but can learn from others mistakes and even history's successes and failures is key. I remember complaining to my dad once when I felt like nothing was going my way and everything seemed harder then what my friends were going through. I felt like I was learning ten lessons for every one my friends were. My dad just simply said, "You aren't expecting the same result so why are you expecting the same process? You are called to leadership and to affect the world in huge ways. That means God is going to take you through a different process to develop, you and if that seems harder then so be it." It was so comforting to understand that I wanted a big destiny, so there was a different price to pay. As a parent, you are going to have to help your child not compare themselves, especially to the world. When they get frustrated, sometimes it might be the frustration centered around comparison!

Teaching Point 9

GOD CAN SHOW YOU WHAT IS POSSIBLE THROUGH OTHERS

GOD CAN SHOW YOU WHAT IS POSSIBLE THROUGH OTHERS

TEACHING POINT 9

1. Biblical Foundations 3.3:
"God Will Do The Same for You"
2. Student Key Verse: John 14:12
3. Teaching Content 9
4. Student Question: *What examples have you seen in your own life and in your friends' lives to prove that God wants to bless everyone with a close connection to His heart?*

3.3 BIBLICAL FOUNDATIONS: GOD WILL DO THE SAME FOR YOU

Acts 10:34-35: "Peter fairly exploded with his good news: 'It's God's own truth, nothing could be plainer: God plays no favorites! It makes no difference who you are or where you're from—if you want God and are ready to do as he says, the door is open.'" Peter was sharing to a crowd of people who thought God was only going to move for the Jewish people. He was sharing the message that God loves each one of us and that what He will do for one, He will do for any who choose Him. If you see people who have been given something by their heavenly Father, you can pray and ask God to do it for you as well. Romans 2:11 says, "For there is no partiality with God" (Romans 2:11 NASB). God will do the same thing for Thomas and you!

Student Key Verse

John 14:12: "I, on my way to the Father, am giving you the same work to do that I've been doing. You can count on it."

GOD CAN SHOW YOU WHAT IS POSSIBLE THROUGH OTHERS

It is possible to be like Jesus, because He even said you will do greater works than He did. "Believe me: I am in my Father and my Father is in me. If you can't believe that, believe what you see—these works. The person who trusts me will not only do what I'm doing but even greater things, because I, on my way to the Father, am giving you the same work to do that I've been doing. You can count on it" (John 14:11-12).

Brothers and sisters always want to have what's fair, and parents try their hardest to make sure that they never give more to one child than another. Because we're all God's children, when you see God doing something for someone else, it gives you a receipt that you can cash in with the Father. You should always want the same benefits you see others getting, even if that benefit will end up making your life turn out differently than your friends' lives. Every benefit God gives you will still be super valuable.

Romans 2:11: "God doesn't give based on where you are from or how you were brought up." God doesn't play favorites. He doesn't like one of us more than another. He doesn't do something for one of His kids that He isn't willing to do for another. He didn't just send Jesus for some of us! He sent Him for all of us, so we could all be restored to Him! This means you have full access to what God wants to provide for you. You should get spiritually hungry for what God has done for your friends so he can do it for you.

Teacher Notes

Student Question/Reflection

What examples have you seen in your own life and in your friends' lives to prove that God wants to bless everyone with a close connection to His heart? When you find it hard to trust God, what do you do to stay connected to His love?

QUESTION/REFLECTION

Question/Reflection

What examples have you seen in your own life and in your friends' lives to prove that God wants to bless everyone with a close connection to his heart?

WORKBOOK CHAPTER 3 55

_____

_____

_____

TIP FOR PARENTS:

One of the things most kids don't know is the love you invest in them when you give them something. Tell your child/children the thing you did for them or bought them (or vacation you took them on) that was your favorite thing you ever did for them. Tell them about the planning and excitement or price behind it. Then draw a parallel to God the Father and Jesus. It is so important that your kids can relate to the sacrifices you are making for them because you love them, but they won't be able to if you don't spend time sharing vulnerably about those sacrifices.

I remember our favorite Christmas: we seemed to get the most presents that year, and although most were not on our direct Christmas list, they were so enjoyable! A few years later, my mom shared with us about how they had no money that Christmas, and had no idea how they were going to make Christmas happen. She even told my oldest sister, who was eleven years older, that they couldn't get her anything, but that they would make it up afterwards. She was so gracious. She understood. They prayed together and asked God to do a miracle. Then, on Christmas Eve, my parents received a check they weren't expecting, and on top of that, when my mom took my older sister shopping for all of us (including her) for Christmas presents, everything was on the best sale she had ever seen. It ended up being our favorite Christmas, and we didn't even know the backstory! When we heard that (we were ten and thirteen), it caused us to have even more connection and respect for our parents. The power of your vulnerable story, after the fact, can mean the world to your child (not during, which can give them a sense of insecurity).

ACTIVATION

INDIVIDUAL ACTIVITY AND INSTRUCTION

Read example 1 and choose a person who fits the description. Write their name in box 1 and tell why you chose them. Do numbers 2 and 3 the same way.

1) Someone who has a career you'd like to have someday, or someone who is happy in a career the way you want to be. Write down what inspires and excites you about that job.

2) Someone who loves God the way you want to love God.

3) The person who has impacted you the most in your life.

Now turn on a worship song and let God encourage your heart for five minutes about all the awesome ways He will help you be you. He's already done it for the three people you listed. Imagine who you get to be as you grow in God.

_____

_____

_____

_____

_____

_____

_____

_____

_____

_____

ACTIVATION, CONTINUED...

GROUP ACTIVITY AND INSTRUCTION

Have three of the group members share what their hobbies are. Then have three group members share what their favorite type of movie or TV show is. Then have three members share about the way they became a Christian. Isn't it amazing that our processes are completely different and yet we are all the same?

_____

_____

_____

_____

_____

_____

_____

_____

_____

_____

_____

_____

_____

_____

GROWTH PRAYER

God, I know that You always have a full picture in mind when You tell me something, and I trust You! My process may be different from everyone else's, but it is because You and I want a different result! When I see You bless someone else with heart growth or an opportunity to grow toward seeing their dream come true, help me to want and believe that You will do the same for me too.

Amen!

It's time to grow up with God!

ACTIVATION PAGE
GOD WANTS TO SPEAK TO ME!

Try some listening prayer. In the first box, write down something you think you hear God saying to you. In the second box, write down the name of a friend, parent, or family member. Ask God to tell you something about that person. Write what He says into that box, too.

Scripture: Anyone who looks will see, anyone who listens will hear. - Isaiah 32:1-8

PRINTABLE ACTIVATION PAGE AVAILABLE IN TEACHER REPRODUCIBLE PAGES - PAGE 241

PRINTABLE COLORING PAGE AVAILABLE IN TEACHER REPRODUCIBLE PAGES - PAGE 241

CHAPTER 4 CHECKLIST

- ☐ Read Chapter 4 in *Growing Up with God*
- ☐ Choose DVD – Option One or Two
- ☐ Read aloud: Student testimonials
- ☐ Review with Students: Synopsis

TEACHING POINT 10:
RECOGNIZE THE PRESENCE OF GOD AND TAKE CHANCES

- ☐ Teach / Review Biblical Foundations
  Biblical Foundations 4.1:
  "Promises Aren't Always Free"
- ☐ Share: Student Key Verse
  Matthew 5:14
- ☐ Teach / Review: Teaching Content 10
  Recognize the presence of God and take chances
- ☐ Student Question / Reflection
  Is there anything you are afraid might happen if you are brave and do what God asks you to do? What would make you less afraid?

TEACHING POINT 11:
TAKE SMALL STEPS OF RISK TO START GROWING

- ☐ Teach / Review Biblical Foundations
  Biblical Foundations 4.2:
  "Grow by Steps"
- ☐ Share: Student Key Verse
  James 1:16
- ☐ Teach / Review: Teaching Content 11
  Take small steps of risk to start growing
- ☐ Student Question / Reflection
  What small steps can you take this week that will help you grow in love? If you have already done some kind acts, what difference have you seen them make in the lives of those around you?

TEACHING POINT 12:
BE ON THE LOOKOUT FOR WAYS TO APPLY WORDS TO CURRENT CIRCUMSTANCES

- ☐ Teach / Review Biblical Foundations
  Biblical Foundations 4.3:
  "Waiting on Him"
- ☐ Share: Student Key Verse
  Colossians 3:12-14
- ☐ Teach / Review: Teaching Content 12
  Be on the lookout for ways to apply words to current circumstances
- ☐ Student Question / Reflection
  When you look at your Christian friends' lives, when do you see them acting like Jesus? How do you think they grow into being more like Him?

PRAY GROWTH PRAYER

GROWTH ACTIVITIES

- ☐ Individual
- ☐ Group
- ☐ Activity Page
- ☐ Coloring Page
- ☐ Implement parenting tip into weekly life

Growing Up with God

CHAPTER

4

TEACHER GUIDE - CHAPTER 4 OVERVIEW

CHAPTER 4 OVERVIEW

☐ Teaching Overview   ☐ DVD Session 4

☐ Chapter Synopsis   ☐ Growth Prayer

TEACHING POINT 10:
RECOGNIZE THE PRESENCE OF GOD AND TAKE CHANCES

1. Biblical Foundations 4.1:
"Promises Aren't Always Free"

2. Student Key Verse: Matthew 5:14

3. Teaching Content 10

4. Student Question: *Is there anything you are afraid might happen if you are brave and do what God asks you to do? What would make you less afraid?*

TEACHING POINT 12:
BE ON THE LOOKOUT FOR WAYS TO APPLY WORDS TO CURRENT CIRCUMSTANCES

1. Biblical Foundations 4.3:
"Waiting on Him"

2. Student Key Verse: Colossians 3:12-14

3. Teaching Content 12

4. Student Question: *When you look at your Christian friends' lives, when do you see them acting like Jesus? How do you think they grow into being more like Him?*

TEACHING POINT 11:
TAKE SMALL STEPS OF RISK TO START GROWING

1. Biblical Foundations 4.2:
"Grow By Steps"

2. Student Key Verse: James 1:16

3. Teaching Content 11

4. Student Question: *What small steps can you take this week that will help you grow in love? If you have already done some kind acts, what difference have you seen them make in the lives of those around you?*

GROWTH ACTIVITIES

1. Individual
2. Group
3. Activity Page
4. Coloring Page
5. Growth Prayer

STORY SYNOPSIS

Lucas goes to the first soccer practice of the season. The kids start picking on a new kid, and Lucas feels he has to intervene. He does, but then the bully starts making fun of Lucas and pushes him to the ground as well. It doesn't bother Lucas, but later as he talks to the new kid, Jamal, he starts to feel the presence of the Holy Spirit. He thinks that his word from God about having a brother might apply to a new friendship with Jamal. This seems strange to him because he doesn't even know Jamal.

Lucas takes a risk on what he thinks the word means. He asks Jamal to hang out even though Jamal isn't normally someone Lucas would have chosen as a friend. After the conversation, Lucas spends a lot of time thinking about what God is going to do next.

CHILD'S TESTIMONY

Will's Story, Age 9

There was a kid at school who kept bullying me. We did everything: my parents talked to the principal and the teacher's and they talked to his parents. Then one day God gave me a vision of who he was and I saw him the way God loves him. I felt like God said he loved the same kinds of books I did. So I brought one to school the next day with a note that said, "I forgive you for being mean to me and hope that you enjoy this book. I am a Christian and asked God what you liked, and I felt like he told me this book was something you liked, so I wanted to give it you. This is my favorite book series, so if you want to talk about it later, we can."

He told me the next day that he had been wanting that book forever and we ended up talking all about it. Now he is my best friend, and I know—from him telling me—that he had been going through a real hard time in life when he was being mean to me.

LET'S GET STARTED

Let's jump right into Chapter 4! If you have elected to have your students read each chapter as they go along with the DVDs, then now is the time to read Chapter 4 in *Growing Up with God*. If your students are reading their book outside of your class setting, then please skip down to the teaching points.

PLAY DVD SESSION 4

OPTION 1:

Watch entire Session four and go back and review all three Teaching Points together.

OPTION 2:

1. Watch the Chapter four synopsis, Shawn's engaging story, and Teaching Point ten.
2. Pause the DVD for Student Question/Reflection activity.
3. Resume DVD for Teaching Point eleven.
4. Pause the DVD for Student Question/Reflection activity.
5. Resume DVD for Teaching Point twelve.
6. Pause the DVD for Student Question/Reflection activity.

GROWTH PRAYER
PRAY ALONG WITH SHAWN ON THE DVD GROWTH PRAYER

God, I pray that I would learn how to recognize your presence. I pray that you would give me the courage to take chances on what I think you're saying, even when it costs me something! Help me take risks so that I can really grow. Help me to know how to apply your Bible, and words you have given me, to my everyday life.

Amen!

Teacher Notes:

_____

_____

_____

_____

_____

_____

_____

_____

Teaching Point 10

RECOGNIZE THE PRESENCE OF GOD AND TAKE CHANCES

Page 64

RECOGNIZE THE PRESENCE OF GOD AND TAKE CHANCES

TEACHING POINT 10

1. Biblical Foundations 4.1:
"Promises Aren't Always Free"
2. Student Key Verse: Matthew 5:14
3. Teaching Content 10
4. Student Question: *Is there anything you are afraid might happen if you are brave and do what God asks you to do? What would make you less afraid?*

4.1 BIBLICAL FOUNDATIONS: PROMISES AREN'T ALWAYS FREE

Moses (in the Bible) was in charge of leading the children of God from Egypt into the Promised Land. It wasn't easy. God's people needed to leave their home and start over in a foreign land. They paid a big price leaving what they knew to go into the unknown. The presence of God was with them and they were willing to take a chance. With each step of the unknown, they stepped into the promises that God had for them. "Moses spoke to the people: 'Don't be afraid. Stand firm and watch God do his work of salvation for you today. Take a good look at the Egyptians today for you're never going to see them again'" (Exodus 14:13).

Student Key Verse

Matthew 5:14: "You're here to be light, bringing out the God-colors in the world."

Teacher Notes

RECOGNIZE THE PRESENCE OF GOD AND TAKE CHANCES

Learning how to grow in your relationship with God happens at all times. You learn as much through your time with other kids or on projects as you do when you are praying or at a church meeting. It is good to process your day with God every night before you go to bed. Is there anything He is highlighting to you that you did well in? Celebrate that and thank God for it. Was there anything you regret that you did or said? Just say sorry to God and think about how you will do it differently next time. Dwell on what was good throughout your day or week.

Sometimes doing things God's told you to do, through the Holy Spirit or the Bible, can cost you something. You have to take chances that not every other kid would take, like befriending a bullied kid or helping someone through a hard time. Jesus was always doing this. He was the most important person on earth, and yet He stopped to play with kids and hang out with people no one else would. He was a friend to everyone.

Jesus preached one of His most amazing messages about you: "Let me tell you why you are here. You're here to be salt-seasoning that brings out the God-flavors of this earth. If you lose your saltiness, how will people taste godliness? . . . You're here to be light, bringing out the God-colors in the world. God is not a secret to be kept. . . . Be generous with your lives. By opening up to others, you'll prompt people to open up with God, this generous Father in heaven" (Matthew 5:13-16).

You are called to show the world what He is like. Sometimes this means taking a risk by spending time with someone who no one else will spend time with, or by doing something nice for someone when you don't even know him or her. When you are a light like this, God causes you to shine from brighter and brighter places, and He is so proud of you.

Student Question/Reflection

Is there anything you are afraid might happen if you are brave and do what God asks you to do? What would make you less afraid?

QUESTION/REFLECTION

Question/Reflection

Is there anything you are afraid might happen if you are brave and do what God asks you to do? What would make you less afraid?

WORKBOOK CHAPTER 4 67

_____

_____

_____

_____

_____

_____

TIP FOR PARENTS:

It is important for your kids to connect to you by seeing your relationship with God in your moments of strength and weaknesses. We learn as much about the disciples in hearing about their mistakes as we do by seeing their successes—like Peter falling as he walked on water, or James and John asking if they could sit at the right and left hand of Jesus when He became king. We learn great character by seeing how other people work through their character issues. Think about something in your spiritual journey that you took a risk and failed on, or that didn't work out the way you had hoped. What did you learn from it? How did it change you? After that, how did you believe that God would do what He told you the next time? Your children would love to hear one of these stories while they are growing in taking on challenges and risks in their own faith. I remember when I was eleven, I was trying to share my faith and it was going awfully. I felt like I would never successfully introduce anyone else to Jesus. My mom shared with me how it took her three years of sharing Jesus with people before someone got saved, and a lot of that process for her was that she needed to learn how to share her faith. She actually began to develop her faith and relational skills. This helped me so much because I had only done it, like, four times, and to hear how much it didn't work for her, but that she kept trying, gave me courage.

Teaching Point 11

TAKE SMALL STEPS OF RISK TO START GROWING

TAKE SMALL STEPS OF RISK TO START GROWING

TEACHING POINT 11

1. Biblical Foundations 4.2:
"Grow By Steps"
2. Student Key Verse: James 1:16
3. Teaching Content 11
4. Student Question: *What small steps can you take this week that will help you grow in love? If you have already done some kind acts, what difference have you seen them make in the lives of those around you?*

4.2 BIBLICAL FOUNDATIONS: GROW BY STEPS

Peter, a disciple of Jesus, was on a boat in the middle of the night. He saw a person walking on the water, but he did not know it was Jesus. Peter knew if it was Jesus, then he would be comforted by Him. So Peter said, "If it is You, Jesus, call me to You." Jesus replied, "Come ahead." Peter jumped out of the boat toward Jesus in the water! Amazing! Peter took one step at a time walking towards Jesus while walking on the water. He only started to sink when he looked down. However, when he was looking into the eyes of Jesus, he was able to do the impossible! Take one step at a time looking into Jesus's eyes.

"Peter, suddenly bold, said, 'Master, if it's really you, call me to come to you on the water.' He said, 'Come ahead.' Jumping out of the boat, Peter walked on the water to Jesus. But when he looked down at the waves churning beneath his feet, he lost his nerve and started to sink. He cried, 'Master, save me!' Jesus didn't hesitate. He reached down and grabbed his hand. Then he said, 'Faint-heart, what got into you?'" — Matthew 14:28–31

Student Key Verse

James 1:16: "So, my very dear friends, don't get thrown off course."

TAKE SMALL STEPS OF RISK TO START GROWING

When you are learning how to walk with God and hear His voice, you just have to take one step at a time. We all have to start somewhere. If you heard God say you are called to love homeless people, maybe your mom can help you pack a lunch for a homeless person you see sometimes and bring it to him. The only way to grow in faith is by action.

James talks about this: "Dear friends, do you think you'll get anywhere in this if you learn all the right words but never do anything? Does merely talking about faith indicate that a person really has it? For instance, you come upon an old friend dressed in rags and half-starved and say, 'Good morning, friend! Be clothed in Christ! Be filled with the Holy Spirit!' and walk off without providing so much as a coat or a cup of soup—where does that get you? Isn't it obvious that God-talk without God-acts is outrageous nonsense? . . . You can no more show me your works apart from your faith than I can show you my faith apart from my works. Faith and works, works and faith, fit together hand in glove" (James 2:14-17).

When God speaks to you and when you do what He says, you should be able to track the difference He's made in your life. You should be able to see the difference you are making in the world around you. Maybe it's as simple as an act of service for your parents by doing dishes or walking the dog. Maybe it's as intense as joining a program at school to volunteer with disabled kids. The reality is that you will only grow in God when you take steps of faith to do something that comes out of your relationship with Him. Lots of people say they are mature in their relationship with God because they know a lot, but knowing a lot without a friendship with God is a dead relationship.

Student
Question/Reflection

What small steps can you take this week that will help you grow in love?
If you have already done some kind acts, what difference have you seen
them make in the lives of those around you?

_____

_____

_____

_____

_____

_____

QUESTION/REFLECTION

Question/Reflection

What small steps can you take this week that will
help you grow in love? If you have already done some
kind acts, what difference have you seen them make
in the lives of those around you?

_____

_____

_____

_____

_____

_____

_____

_____

_____

_____

WORKBOOK CHAPTER 4 **71**

Teaching Point 12

BE ON THE LOOKOUT FOR WAYS TO APPLY WORDS TO CURRENT CIRCUMSTANCES

BE ON THE LOOKOUT FOR WAYS TO APPLY WORDS TO CURRENT CIRCUMSTANCES

TEACHING POINT 12

1. Biblical Foundations 4.3:
"Waiting on Him"

2. Student Key Verse: Colossians 3:12-14

3. Teaching Content 12

4. Student Question: *When you look at your Christian friends' lives, when do you see them acting like Jesus? How do you think they grow into being more like Him?*

4.3 BIBLICAL FOUNDATIONS: WAITING ON HIM

Waiting on God helps us listen to His voice. If we are always talking and never give God a chance to talk, then we are missing out on relationship. We can hear His voice so much better when we become still, are patient, and wait on Him. Waiting allows us to climb high in our thoughts and heart to scan for what he is saying. Purse His voice by waiting on Him. "I'll climb to the lookout tower and scan the horizon. I'll wait to see what God says" (Habakkuk 2:1).

Student Key Verse

Colossians 3:12-14: "Regardless of what else you put on, wear love. It's your basic, all-purpose garment. Never be without it."

Teacher Notes

BE ON THE LOOKOUT FOR WAYS TO APPLY WORDS TO CURRENT CIRCUMSTANCES

The Bible is awesome because it teaches you how to thrive in life. Hearing God's voice and walking with Him in friendship will teach you how to be the greatest version of yourself that you were meant to be!

You have to learn to apply what He is saying to your life, though. When you are reading the Bible or listening to God and He shows you something about yourself or the world around you, write it down. Then look for it happening in your everyday life.

"So, chosen by God for this new life of love, dress in the wardrobe God picked out for you: compassion, kindness, humility, quiet strength, discipline. Be even-tempered, content with second place, quick to forgive an offense. . . . And regardless of what else you put on, wear love. It's your basic, all-purpose garment. Never be without it" (Colossians 3:12-14).

Is He telling you that He is going to teach you about leadership? Look for ways to be a leader at school or with friends, in ideas or activities. Do you care about making things fair for people who are down on their luck? Jesus always stood up for the outcast. Look for ways to be kind to people that other people ignore. As you do these things, you will definitely begin to understand how God is moving around you and in you to form His love in you.

Student Question/Reflection

When you look at your Christian friends' lives, when do you see them acting like Jesus? How do you think they grow into being more like him?

What do you think Matthew 5 means: "You're here . . . to bring out the God-flavors in the earth," or "to bring out the God-colors in the world"?

QUESTION/REFLECTION

Question/Reflection

When you look at your Christian friends' lives, when do you see them acting like Jesus? How do you think they grow into being more like him?

WORKBOOK CHAPTER 4 75

_____

_____

_____

_____

_____

_____

TIP FOR PARENTS:

It is amazing when you can teach your child how to apply words to their life. This can start even before they receive prophecies or hear God's voice. You can start by sharing how the Bible applies to their lives. Get a great devotional to do with them daily for a while, with the goal of applying what you are reading to life together! Your children learning how to read the Bible in a way that causes them to filter their life through it is essential to growing into maturity! I remember my mom doing a devotional with us for a few weeks when I was young, and it laid a foundation that I still remember. Think about it — people read fortune cookies, horoscopes, and all kinds of things trying to find messages for life. We have the Bible and can teach our children exactly how to apply it to life to glean wisdom, life direction, character growth, and love!

ACTIVATION

INDIVIDUAL ACTIVITY AND INSTRUCTION

Take a risk: Talk to someone and share something encouraging! Find someone who is safe for you to talk to and share something incredibly kind or encouraging. It can be a spiritual word or just a natural encouragement, for example: "Your smile makes the whole room feel happy," or "The way you keep trying makes me want to try harder too. Thank you."

ACTIVATION, CONTINUED...

GROUP ACTIVITY AND INSTRUCTION

Have volunteers take it in turns to be in the middle of the group. These should be people who feel like God has shown them something they are going to do in life but they haven't started yet, or who have something that they want to do. Now have everyone else do listening prayer (including them) to ask God what some steps or what a strategy might be to start doing that thing. Try not to give just good advice; ask Jesus!

_____

_____

_____

_____

_____

_____

_____

_____

_____

_____

_____

GROWTH PRAYER

God, I pray that I would learn how to recognize Your presence. I pray that You would give me the courage to take chances on what I think You're saying, even when it costs me something! Help me take risks so that I can really grow. Help me to know how to apply Your Bible, and words You have given me, to my everyday life.

Amen!

ACTIVATION PAGE
MY CALLING AND THE STEPS TO GET THERE

In the box at the bottom of Jamal's ladder, write down one or more of the things you are called to. Examples: "I am called to act." "I am called to preach." "I am called to be a policeman." "I am called to worship." "I am called to teach."

1. On the first rung of the ladder, write something you know you'll need to do to fulfill your calling (like a specific training class you can go to).

2. On the second ladder rung, write down a step you have seen someone else take toward the same calling—because learning from others' lives helps us to pursue our own calling.

3. On the third rung, ask God to show you one step you can take now toward fulfilling your calling. Keep asking for steps and see how many he will give you up the ladder!

Scripture: Strength! Courage! Don't be timid; don't get discouraged. God, your God, is with you every step you take. – Joshua 1:9

PRINTABLE ACTIVATION PAGE AVAILABLE IN TEACHER REPRODUCIBLE PAGES · PAGE 241

PRINTABLE COLORING PAGE AVAILABLE IN TEACHER REPRODUCIBLE PAGES - PAGE 241

CHAPTER 5 CHECKLIST

- ☐ Read Chapter 5 in *Growing Up with God*
- ☐ Choose DVD – Option One or Two
- ☐ Read aloud: Student testimonials
- ☐ Review with Students: Synopsis

TEACHING POINT 13:
SOMETIMES GOD LEADS YOU TO YOUR GOALS IN INDIRECT WAYS

- ☐ Teach / Review Biblical Foundations
  Biblical Foundations 5.1:
  "God Is Our Guide"
- ☐ Share: Student Key Verse
  1 Corinthians 13:2
- ☐ Teach / Review: Teaching Content 13
  Sometimes God leads you to your goals in indirect ways
- ☐ Student Question / Reflection
  How does it feel different in your heart when you do things for your parents out of obedience compared to when you do things for them out of love? Which way makes you feel more connected?

TEACHING POINT 14:
SOMETIMES LIFE HAS OBSTACLES IN THE WAY OF YOUR PROMISES

- ☐ Teach / Review Biblical Foundations
  Biblical Foundations 5.2:
  "Never Give Up"
- ☐ Share: Student Key Verse
  James 1:2
- ☐ Teach / Review: Teaching Content 14
  Sometimes life has obstacles in the way of your promises
- ☐ Student Question / Reflection
  Was there ever a time when it looked like God wasn't doing what He'd promised, but then it turned out He was making it happen all along?

TEACHING POINT 15:
YOU ARE ALWAYS CALLED TO THE WHO, NOT THE WHAT

- ☐ Teach / Review Biblical Foundations
  Biblical Foundations 5.3:
  "People Are Our Destiny"
- ☐ Share: Student Key Verse
  1 John 3:18
- ☐ Teach / Review: Teaching Content 15
  You are always called to the who, not the what
- ☐ Student Question / Reflection
  If you did nothing the right way ever again, would God still love you and want to bless you? (See Ephesians 2:8-10) That's the kind of love He wants to give you for other people.

PRAY GROWTH PRAYER

GROWTH ACTIVITIES

- ☐ Individual
- ☐ Group
- ☐ Activity Page
- ☐ Coloring Page
- ☐ Implement parenting tip into weekly life

Growing Up with God
CHAPTER
5

TEACHER GUIDE - CHAPTER 5 OVERVIEW

CHAPTER 5 OVERVIEW

☐ Teaching Overview   ☐ DVD Session 5

☐ Chapter Synopsis   ☐ Growth Prayer

TEACHING POINT 13:
SOMETIMES GOD LEADS YOU TO YOUR GOALS IN INDIRECT WAYS

1. Biblical Foundations 5.1:

"God Is Our Guide"

2. Student Key Verse: 1 Corinthians 13:2

3. Teaching Content 13

4. Student Question: *How does it feel different in your heart when you do things for your parents out of obedience compared to when you do things for them out of love? Which way makes you feel more connected?*

TEACHING POINT 15:
YOU ARE ALWAYS CALLED TO THE WHO, NOT THE WHAT

1. Biblical Foundations 5.3:

"People Are Our Destiny"

2. Student Key Verse: 1 John 3:18

3. Teaching Content 15

4. Student Question: *If you did nothing the right way ever again, would God still love you and want to bless you? (See Ephesians 2:8-10) That's the kind of love he wants to give you for other people.*

TEACHING POINT 14:
SOMETIMES LIFE HAS OBSTACLES IN THE WAY OF YOUR PROMISES

1. Biblical Foundations 5.2:

"Never Give Up"

2. Student Key Verse: James 1:2

3. Teaching Content 14

4. Student Question: *Was there ever a time when it looked like God wasn't doing what He'd promised, but then it turned out He was making it happen all along?*

GROWTH ACTIVITIES

1. Individual
2. Group
3. Activity Page
4. Coloring Page
5. Growth Prayer

STORY SYNOPSIS

Maria finds out she and Harper are going to be in a show choir, not just a normal choir. Also a teacher has moved from New York City to host a musical in the theater next season. They will need kid actors for it, and their choir group will get to audition. Maria feels like it's her chance to be a real actress, and Harper is just as excited as Maria is about God's word to her coming true.

Maria sings really well, but then competition comes in the form of a very professional girl, Brooke, who has been singing and acting for years. Maria is devastated because there is only one lead role, and Brooke will probably get it. When Maria talks to God about her dream and word, she sees that to God, acting is not her destiny; the people she gets to love through acting are her destiny. She gets to love like Jesus loved.

CHILD'S TESTIMONY

Burt's Testimony, a Grown-Up

I often take the entire children's ministry out to walk the neighborhood and pray. One particularly beautiful Sunday morning, I had the kids line up, gave them instructions, and off they went. The children had been practicing hearing from God and activating their faith and spiritual gifts. As they walked through a few blocks, praying for the city and the families that lived in the homes they were passing, they adamantly began asking to stop at this one particular house. To me, this house appeared no different than the rest. The children insisted they wanted to knock on the door and pray for whomever answered. They were compelled to give a blessing to the people inside.

I knocked at the door and a woman answered. After explaining what we had been doing and why we were there, the woman asked the children if they wanted to come inside. She allowed them to walk around and pray for God's love and safety to fill the house. After hearing their prayers, she was very moved and confided the house's true purpose. It was a secret safe place for children whose own homes weren't a safe place to be anymore. We loved that a very present and sovereign God cares for children so much that He would make sure they had a safe place to go to. It was a powerful encounter shared with that woman, the children, and our leadership team. It was incredible to see such innocent children used so easily to bring hope to a house where scared children could be safe.

LET'S GET STARTED

Let's jump right into Chapter 5! If you have elected to have your students read each chapter as they go along with the DVDs, then now is the time to read Chapter 5 in *Growing Up with God*. If your students are reading their book outside of your class setting, then please skip down to the teaching points.

PLAY DVD SESSION 5

OPTION 1:

Watch entire Session five and go back and review all three Teaching Points together.

OPTION 2:

1. Watch the Chapter five synopsis, Shawn's engaging story, and Teaching Point thirteen.
2. Pause the DVD for Student Question/ Reflection activity.
3. Resume DVD for Teaching Point fourteen.
4. Pause the DVD for Student Question/ Reflection activity.
5. Resume DVD for Teaching Point fifteen.
6. Pause the DVD for Student Question/ Reflection activity.

GROWTH PRAYER
PRAY ALONG WITH SHAWN ON THE DVD GROWTH PRAYER

God, when I am pursuing You, help me to trust that You are leading me even when it doesn't feel direct! Help me to understand how to overcome any obstacle that is in front of my spiritual promises! Help me to see the ones I get to love...show me who they are... not just what I am supposed to do for You.

Amen!

It's time to go out there and practice so you can grow!

Teacher Notes:

_____

_____

_____

_____

_____

_____

_____

_____

Teaching Point 13

SOMETIMES GOD LEADS YOU TO YOUR GOALS IN INDIRECT WAYS

SOMETIMES GOD LEADS YOU TO YOUR GOALS IN INDIRECT WAYS

TEACHING POINT 13

1. Biblical Foundations 5.1:
"God Is Our Guide"
2. Student Key Verse: 1 Corinthians 13:2
3. Teaching Content 13
4. Student Question: *How does it feel different in your heart when you do things for your parents out of obedience compared to when you do things for them out of love? Which way makes you feel more connected?*

5.1 BIBLICAL FOUNDATIONS: GOD IS OUR GUIDE

God sees and knows everything. We only see a little of what there is to see. However, God is faithful to lead us and take us to places that we haven't seen before. Our life may be a journey that we did not plan or expect! The places we go, the friends that we have, and the people in our family may all be unique and different from what we would say is normal. Thankfully, God has a purpose for us. He holds our hand and guides us in the best way possible. When we trust Him, we are accomplishing our goals! "But when the Friend comes, the Spirit of the Truth, he will take you by the hand and guide you into all the truth there is" (John 16:13).

Student Key Verse

1 Corinthians 13:2: "If I speak God's Word with power, revealing all his mysteries and making everything plain as day, and if I have faith that says to a mountain, 'Jump,' and it jumps, but I don't love, I'm nothing"

SOMETIMES GOD LEADS YOU TO YOUR GOALS IN INDIRECT WAYS

Many times when God talks to you, you don't know exactly what He means until you watch Him make it happen in your life. When He tells you something, He's not just informing you of it. He wants to give you the ability to be like Him. He wants to teach you how to be amazing and how to make awesome choices. If you only do all the right things for Him, you are more of a servant than a son or daughter. God doesn't just want servants who know how to do all the right things. He wants sons and daughters who know how to make powerful decisions that make their Father in heaven look amazing!

"If I speak with human eloquence and angelic ecstasy but don't love, I'm nothing but the creaking of a rusty gate. If I speak God's Word with power, revealing all his mysteries and making everything plain as day, and if I have faith that says to a mountain, 'Jump,' and it jumps, but I don't love, I'm nothing" (1 Corinthians 13:1-2). So if you know how to do all the right things because you have all the right principles, it's not enough. He wants you to be really connected to His heart of love because that is when you know you are really living and growing in God.

This is why Jesus told parables and stories instead of just telling people what to do. He didn't want servants; He wanted co-heirs. He wanted to give His Father sons and daughters, not just slaves, so He told them stories that would make the kingdom come alive inside them instead of just giving them rules they could follow.

Teacher Notes

Student
Question/Reflection

How does it feel different in your heart when you do things for your parents out of obedience compared to when you do things for them out of love? Which way makes you feel more connected?

_____

_____

_____

_____

_____

_____

_____

_____

_____

_____

_____

_____

_____

_____

_____

_____

QUESTION/REFLECTION

Question/Reflection

How does it feel different in your heart when you do things for your parents out of obedience compared to when you do things for them out of love? Which way makes you feel more connected?

WORKBOOK CHAPTER 5 87

Teaching Point 14

SOMETIMES LIFE HAS OBSTACLES IN THE WAY OF YOUR PROMISES

SOMETIMES LIFE HAS OBSTACLES IN THE WAY OF YOUR PROMISES

TEACHING POINT 14

1. Biblical Foundations 5.2:
"Never Give Up"

2. Student Key Verse: James 1:2

3. Teaching Content 14

4. Student Question: *Was there ever a time when it looked like God wasn't doing what He'd promised, but then it turned out He was making it happen all along?*

5.2 BIBLICAL FOUNDATIONS: NEVER GIVE UP

King David (in the Bible) had some obstacles in his way before he became king. Most of us remember the giant, Goliath, that young David needed to conquer. Even before David fought Goliath, he fought with a lion and a bear to protect his father's sheep. Each and every obstacle was a stepping stone for David to step into his spiritual promises. Never give up. God will support you to make your dreams come true!

"God, who delivered me from the teeth of the lion and the claws of the bear, will deliver me from this Philistine." — 1 Samuel 17:37

Student Key Verse

James 1:2 (NIV): "Consider it pure joy, my brothers and sisters, whenever you face trials of many kinds."

SOMETIMES LIFE HAS OBSTACLES IN THE WAY OF YOUR PROMISES

When you hear from God about something in your future or about your life purpose, there will inevitably be obstacles that get in the way of that happening. God wants to do things through you that are bigger than you could do based on your own skills, talents, and relational abilities. He also wants to do things in your life for different reasons than you might want. Most people without God want to do amazing things just to have the benefit of having other people tell them they're amazing. If you are an awesome singer, you can make albums and buy a big house and be famous. But when God calls you to amazing things, it's so you can have an amazing impact on the world through His love! You aren't doing it for your own benefit, even though you will benefit. You are doing it for His love, and the end result of you living out your life purpose will look different than it might for others. This happens because living life in God's love will give you treasure in heaven, not just a fulfillment on earth!

Because you are not just doing things for yourself but for God and the world around you, you will experience different obstacles than some people face. If you were doing things to make your life better just for your own satisfaction, you wouldn't have to worry about how your life impacts the people around you. You could even treat people really badly to accomplish more and get what you want, but as a Christian, you're here to do everything in your life to love the world and to honor God! That means that you get to treasure people, but sometimes these very people become obstacles until God unfolds His plan.

Teacher Notes

_____

_____

_____

_____

_____

_____

_____

_____

_____

_____

_____

_____

_____

_____

_____

_____

_____

_____

Student Question/Reflection

Was there ever a time when it looked like God wasn't doing what he'd promised, but then it turned out he was making it happen all along?

QUESTION/REFLECTION

Question/Reflection

Was there ever a time when it looked like God wasn't doing what he'd promised, but then it turned out he was making it happen all along?

WORKBOOK CHAPTER 9   91

_____

_____

_____

_____

_____

_____

_____

TIP FOR PARENTS:

Engaging your children about obstacles and the process of life is so valuable, but sometimes it's hard to do until obstacles arise. Having a conversation about obstacles is so important, though, because all of us face them. Try asking your children about something they are believing to accomplish in life. Then ask them to think about possible obstacles they might face, or that others have faced, when it comes to this dream. Talk about an obstacle that God helped you overcome, and ask them if they have ever noticed God help them overcome something before.

One young girl who came to a camp we were doing told us that her family didn't have money to send her, but she knew she was supposed to come. She prayed and felt God gave her a strategy to raise the money. She asked all of her friends and family to sow a little into registration for the camp instead of throwing her a party or getting her gifts. She got just enough to come, and she knew God was sending her because the strategy worked! Learning about how God wants to help us overcome is such an important topic, and as you lay a foundation now in your talking about it, your kids might just use you as a main sounding board for their process when it comes to harder and harder things.

Teaching Point 15

YOU ARE ALWAYS CALLED TO THE WHO, NOT THE WHAT

YOU ARE ALWAYS CALLED TO THE WHO, NOT THE WHAT

TEACHING POINT 15

1. Biblical Foundations 5.3:
"People Are Our Destiny"
2. Student Key Verse: 1 John 3:18
3. Teaching Content 15
4. Student Question: *If you did nothing the right way ever again, would God still love you and want to bless you? (See Ephesians 2:8-10) That's the kind of love he wants to give you for other people.*

5.3 BIBLICAL FOUNDATIONS: PEOPLE ARE OUR DESTINY

God is so passionate about His people. From the beginning of time, He dreamed of each and every one of us. He desires for us to share in this passionate journey for people. It is easy for us to get caught up thinking about what we should be doing and forget that we are simply called to love. Love those who God gave us. They are our destiny. God is passionate for us. Will you be passionate for His people? "I'll be your God; you'll be my people" (Leviticus 26:12).

 Student Key Verse

I John 3:18: "My dear children, let's not just talk about love; let's practice real love."

YOU ARE ALWAYS CALLED TO THE WHO NOT THE WHAT

Do you know that when Jesus was about to go to the cross, he stressed out beforehand and asked the Father to make it happen another way? But there was no other way. The Father in heaven was good, though, and showed Jesus a vision of everyone who would ever love Him. Hebrews 12:2 says, "For the joy set before him he went to the cross."

You were and are the joy set before Jesus. He was able to go through one of the most brutal sufferings in history because He loved you and wanted to spend eternity with you. You are called to do some amazing things in life, but sometimes you will have to work hard and even persevere through some obstacles. Have you ever asked God to show you the people you get to love so that you can endure anything? When you have love in your heart for the "who" you are performing for, then you can make it through anything! When you are just doing things because you want to perform, then you might lose hope.

John talks about practicing real love when living your life. When you know who you are called to love, you can live a life full of real purpose and you will be truly living. "My dear children, let's not just talk about love; let's practice real love. This is the only way we'll know we're living truly, living in God's reality. . . . We're able to stretch our hands out and receive what we asked for because we're doing what he said, doing what pleases him. Again, this is God's command: to believe in his personally named Son, Jesus Christ. He told us to love each other, in line with the original command. As we keep his commands, we live deeply and surely in him, and he lives in us. And this is how we experience his deep and abiding presence in us: by the Spirit he gave us" (1 John 3:18-24).

Teacher Notes

_____

_____

_____

_____

_____

_____

_____

_____

_____

_____

_____

_____

_____

_____

_____

_____

_____

_____

Student
Question/Reflection

If you did nothing the right way ever again, would God still love you and want to bless you? (See Ephesians 2:8-10) That's the kind of love he wants to give you for other people.

QUESTION/REFLECTION

Question/Reflection

If you did nothing the right way ever again, would God still love you and want to bless you? (See Ephesians 2:8-10.) That's the kind of love he wants to give you for other people.

WORKBOOK CHAPTER 5 95

_____

_____

_____

_____

_____

_____

_____

_____

_____

_____

 ## TIP FOR PARENTS:

After your kids go through this section, a good activation for your family would be to share with each other what you feel called to and who the "who" is for each one of you. Sharing with each other who you are called to love (especially when it is each other) helps you focus on making priorities together, and it also helps you respect each other's decisions.

ACTIVATION

INDIVIDUAL ACTIVITY AND INSTRUCTION

Do you know what you are called to do? If you don't, ask God, your parents, and a friend what they think would be a good fit for you. This might not be the final thing you end up with, but it might give you a good idea. Then ask God which groups of people you will get to love well (write this down), and ask Him for His love for them.

ACTIVATION, CONTINUED...

GROUP ACTIVITY AND INSTRUCTION

Have all the people in your group take turns sharing something they want to do in life — for example, a career, ministry, hobby, or trip. Then think of possible people that they might get to love on or reach through that. Try and see a big picture in your mind of all the people you'll get to love on or reach with your life — so you can see how much love you'll need from God's heart to do it, and see how big His plan is for your life!

GROWTH PRAYER

God, when I am pursuing You, help me to trust that You are leading me even when it doesn't feel direct! Help me to understand how to overcome any obstacle that is in front of my spiritual promises! Help me to see the ones I get to love...show me who they are... not just what I am supposed to do for You.

Amen!

It's time to go out there and practice so you can grow!

ACTIVATION PAGE
WHO IS MY DESTINY!

Who are you called to love? God never puts His light at the bottom of a hill but on the highest place it can shine from! Inside the mountain, write down all the types of people you are called to love to fulfill your destiny. This is where you get to rule in love. For example, if you are called to be a nurse, then you are called to love patients, doctors, other nurses, emergency workers, etc.

Scripture: Live out your God-created identity. Live generously and graciously toward others, the way God lives toward you. – Matthew 5:48

PRINTABLE ACTIVATION PAGE AVAILABLE IN TEACHER REPRODUCIBLE PAGES - PAGE 241

PRINTABLE COLORING PAGE AVAILABLE IN TEACHER REPRODUCIBLE PAGES - PAGE 241

CHAPTER 6 CHECKLIST

- ☐ Read Chapter 6 in *Growing Up with God*
- ☐ Choose DVD – Option One or Two
- ☐ Read aloud: Student testimonials
- ☐ Review with Students: Synopsis

TEACHING POINT 16:
LISTEN TO GOD, EVEN WHEN WHAT HE TELLS YOU TO DO IS HARD

- ☐ Teach / Review Biblical Foundations
  Biblical Foundations 6.1:
  "Recognizing His Voice Builds Friendship"
- ☐ Share: Student Key Verse
  Proverbs 3:6
- ☐ Teach / Review: Teaching Content 16
  Listen to God
- ☐ Student Question / Reflection
  What do you think Matthew 7:13-14 means, to "enter through the narrow gate?" The narrow gate "leads to life, and only a few find it." Why do you think it's so important to Jesus that we do things His way?

TEACHING POINT 17:
TREASURE WHAT GOD TELLS YOU

- ☐ Teach / Review Biblical Foundations
  Biblical Foundations 6.2:
  "You Can Recognize His Voice"
- ☐ Share: Student Key Verse
  John 16:29-30
- ☐ Teach / Review: Teaching Content 17
  Treasure what God tells you
- ☐ Student Question / Reflection
  Sometimes we can get tired waiting for God to do what He's promised. What can you do to keep trusting Him and doing what He wants you to do?

TEACHING POINT 18:
GOD IS ALWAYS TEACHING YOU AND SHARING HIMSELF WITH YOU

- ☐ Teach / Review Biblical Foundations
  Biblical Foundations 6.3:
  "God Is Our Teacher"
- ☐ Share: Student Key Verse
  1 Timothy 4:12
- ☐ Teach / Review: Teaching Content 18
  God is always teaching you and sharing Himself with you
- ☐ Student Question / Reflection
  What are some ways you could spend more time with God and grow your friendship with Him?

PRAY GROWTH PRAYER

GROWTH ACTIVITIES

- ☐ Individual
- ☐ Group
- ☐ Activity Page
- ☐ Coloring Page
- ☐ Implement parenting tip into weekly life

Growing Up with God

CHAPTER

6

TEACHER GUIDE - CHAPTER 6 OVERVIEW

CHAPTER 6 OVERVIEW

- ☐ Teaching Overview
- ☐ Chapter Synopsis
- ☐ DVD Session 6
- ☐ Growth Prayer

TEACHING POINT 16:
LISTEN TO GOD, EVEN WHEN WHAT HE TELLS YOU TO DO IS HARD

1. Biblical Foundations 6.1:
"Recognizing His Voice Builds Friendship"

2. Student Key Verse: Proverbs 3:6

3. Teaching Content 16

4. Student Question: *What do you think Matthew 7:13-14 means, to "enter through the narrow gate?" The narrow gate "leads to life, and only a few find it." Why do you think it's so important to Jesus that we do things His way?*

TEACHING POINT 18:
GOD IS ALWAYS TEACHING YOU AND SHARING HIMSELF WITH YOU

1. Biblical Foundations 6.3:
"God is Our Teacher"

2. Student Key Verse: 1 Timothy 4:12

3. Teaching Content 18

4. Student Question: *What are some ways you could spend more time with God and grow your friendship with Him?*

TEACHING POINT 17:
SEE WHAT HE IS DOING IN OR THROUGH YOUR LIFE

1. Biblical Foundations 6.2:
"You Can Recognize His Voice"

2. Student Key Verse: John 16:29-30

3. Teaching Content 17

4. Student Question: *Sometimes we can get tired waiting for God to do what He's promised. What can you do to keep trusting Him and doing what He wants you to do?*

GROWTH ACTIVITIES

1. Individual
2. Group
3. Activity Page
4. Coloring Page
5. Growth Prayer

STORY SYNOPSIS

Lucas likes Jamal, but none of his friends do because he gets upset easily and never seems to like anyone. Lucas asks God to help him love Jamal well. He's finding it hard to understand why God wants him to be his friend when he's not that easy to be around.

Lucas invites him on a boys' night with his dad, and Jamal has a great time. Afterwards, he shares how he is a foster kid and his home life has been very difficult. Both Lucas and his dad have a strong sense of compassion for him because of his situation. Lucas's parents help Lucas understand that God wants him to see Jamal the way God made him to be, and to look past his flaws. As Christians, we get to do this for everyone. We get to love each other into being the way God designed us to be.

CHILD'S TESTIMONY

Anna's Testimony, Age 9

I saw Jesus in our kitchen. My mommy had taken me and Hudson to the pool that morning, but when we had to leave the pool, I got really mad and yelled at my mom. My mom yelled back at me. After we got home and Mommy was giving us lunch, I told Mommy I was sorry I said mean words that hurt her. I know my words have power and they hurt her heart. Then my mommy asked me why I was grinning, so I told her it was because Jesus just walked in and thanked me for saying I was sorry.

Mommy said, "Jesus is here in the kitchen?" So I said, "Yes, Mommy, He is standing right next to you. Miss Dawn said that you can have Christ-ray vision too, if you try." Mommy said she couldn't see Jesus, so she closed her eyes and said she felt him standing next her. We both started to cry because we were so happy.

LET'S GET STARTED

Let's jump right into Chapter 6! If you have elected to have your students read each chapter as they go along with the DVDs, then now is the time to read Chapter 6 in *Growing Up with God*. If your students are reading their book outside of your class setting, then please skip down to the teaching points.

PLAY DVD SESSION 6

OPTION 1:

Watch entire Session six and go back and review all three Teaching Points together.

OPTION 2:

1. Watch the Chapter six synopsis, Shawn's engaging story, and Teaching Point sixteen.
2. Pause the DVD for Student Question/Reflection activity.
3. Resume DVD for Teaching Point seventeen.
4. Pause the DVD for Student Question/Reflection activity.
5. Resume DVD for Teaching Point eighteen.
6. Pause the DVD for Student Question/Reflection activity.

GROWTH PRAYER
PRAY ALONG WITH SHAWN ON THE DVD GROWTH PRAYER

God, help me to obey You when You ask me to do things, even when it is hard sometimes. Help me to know when You do something in me and through me, because I want to see Your presence and Your love at work in my life. Thank You for sharing Yourself with me. Thank You for teaching me daily how to be like You and how to live an awesome life.

Amen!

Teacher Notes:

_____

_____

_____

_____

_____

_____

_____

_____

Teaching Point 16

LISTEN TO GOD, EVEN WHEN WHAT HE TELLS YOU TO DO IS HARD

LISTEN TO GOD, EVEN WHEN WHAT HE TELLS YOU TO DO IS HARD

TEACHING POINT 16

1. Biblical Foundations 6.1:
"Recognizing His Voice Builds Friendship"
2. Student Key Verse: Proverbs 3:6
3. Teaching Content 16
4. Student Question: *What do you think Matthew 7:13-14 means, to "enter through the narrow gate?" The narrow gate "leads to life, and only a few find it." Why do you think it's so important to Jesus that we do things His way?*

6.1 BIBLICAL FOUNDATIONS: RECOGNIZING HIS VOICE BUILDS FRIENDSHIP

Recognizing God's voice is a process and a journey. Even Jesus's disciples sometimes were confused and did not know that God was talking to them. Jesus is always speaking, sharing, and building friendship with us. He is not silent in any way! He talks to us more than all of our friends combined. As we continue to learn how to hear Him, we can build and grow as we respond back to what He is saying. "'Do you believe in the Son of Man?' The man said, 'Point him out to me, sir, so that I can believe in him.' Jesus said, 'You're looking right at him. Don't you recognize my voice?' 'Master, I believe,' the man said, and worshiped him" (John 9:35–38). "God's Spirit beckons. There are things to do and places to go!" (Romans 8:14)

Student Key Verse

Proverbs 3:6: "Listen for God's voice in everything you do, everywhere you go; he's the one who will keep you on track."

LISTEN TO GOD, EVEN WHEN WHAT HE TELLS YOU TO DO IS HARD

You need to press into listening to God and praying even when it's hard. He is always with you and wants to help you connect to His heart. Sometimes it can be very hard to do what God is asking you to do. Jesus said His road is narrow. This can mean that sometimes it's not easy for you to follow God because there isn't as much freedom for you to be selfish or to just do normal things. If you want a different result, then you have to live a different way.

"Enter through the narrow gate. For wide is the gate and broad is the road that leads to destruction, and many enter through it. But small is the gate and narrow the road that leads to life, and only a few find it. Learning to trust God when we are walking with him is essential!" (Matthew 7:13-14 NIV) "Trust God from the bottom of your heart; don't try to figure out everything on your own. Listen for God's voice in everything you do, everywhere you go; he's the one who will keep you on track" (Proverbs 3:5-6).

When Lucas began to be friends with Jamal, it wasn't easy. Jamal was changing, but it felt slow and other kids didn't want to be around him. Lucas only stayed friends with Jamal because he felt God's love and friendship for him, not because it was extremely satisfying. He was waiting for God to make them like brothers, like He'd promised. It took a while before this happened. Galatians 6:9 says, "Let's not allow ourselves to get fatigued doing good. At the right time we will harvest a good crop if we don't give up, or quit." This means that if you keep going in faith, you will get everything God has promised. It will be like walking in an apple orchard and finding that every apple is ready to be picked and eaten.

You also need to learn how to listen to God's voice encourage you when it is hard. People who just try and do what is right, just because it is right, often miss out on intimacy with God. He wants to encourage you and show you that He is with you.

Teacher Notes

CHAPTER 6   117

Page 105-106

Student Question/Reflection

What do you think Matthew 7:13-14 means, to "enter through the narrow gate?" The narrow gate "leads to life, and only a few find it." Why do you think it's so important to Jesus that we do things his way?

_____

_____

_____

_____

TIP FOR PARENTS:

We need to learn how to listen to our kids when things are hard. Your children will base much of their self-identity on their most immediate environment. If your family life is informed by healthy values, choices, activities, and relationships, they are more likely to internalize those messages as their own.

You can surround your children with healthy people in their immediate social world, people who support everything that goes into the development of a positive self-identity. These healthy messages will not only prime your children to think, feel, and behave in beneficial ways, but they will also provide consistent exposure to contrasting healthy perspectives that can mitigate the influence from media.

Your children have a tremendous capacity to communicate with you about what is happening in their lives—both the good and not so good. Unfortunately, they're often speaking in a language that parents don't understand. If you listen to their messages—verbal, emotional, and behavioral—you'll be better able to hear what they're trying to tell you, particularly when they're asking for help. Also, don't be afraid to talk to your children, especially on topics that make you uncomfortable or they may not want to hear about. Though they may not always seem like they're listening, your children want your guidance and support because they know that they can't go it alone, and they need to know you are on their side.

Teaching Point 17

SEE WHAT HE IS DOING IN AND THROUGH YOUR LIFE

SEE WHAT HE IS DOING IN AND THROUGH YOUR LIFE

TEACHING POINT 17

1. Biblical Foundations 6.2:
"You Can Recognize His Voice"
2. Student Key Verse: John 16:29-30
3. Teaching Content 17
4. Student Question: *Sometimes we can get tired waiting for God to do what He's promised. What can you do to keep trusting Him and doing what He wants you to do?*

6.2 BIBLICAL FOUNDATIONS: YOU CAN RECOGNIZE HIS VOICE

The Father God spoke out of the sky one day. Some thought it was thunder or angels speaking. They did not know it was God talking. As you grow up in God, you begin to mature in your hearing and seeing God. You start to hear God like a father and not like thunder anymore. Realizing the voice that is speaking is not thunder anymore means you can start to recognize what God is saying and doing. You become excited about the possibilities. You recognize God's personality and tendencies. You become accustomed to His love and desire to see more of it.

"A voice came out of the sky: 'I have glorified it, and I'll glorify it again.' The listening crowd said, 'Thunder!' Others said, 'An angel spoke to him!' Jesus said, 'The voice didn't come for me but for you.'" (John 12:28–30)

Student Key Verse

John 16:29–30: "You know all things and that you do not even need to have anyone ask you questions. This makes us believe that you came from God.'"

SEE WHAT HE IS DOING IN OR THROUGH YOUR LIFE

Even the disciples had to learn and grow. Jesus was preaching and telling them stories all the time, and they almost always had to ask Him to explain the meaning behind the stories. He was used to their questions, and often, instead of answering them directly, He actually told them more stories! He wasn't trying to just build their knowledge or intellect. He was teaching them how to see everything through love.

After three years of being with Him, the disciples had grown in love and had formed a heart connection with Him: "His disciples said, 'Finally! You're giving it to us straight, in plain talk—no more figures of speech. Now we know that you know everything—it all comes together in you. You won't have to put up with our questions anymore'" (John 16:29 MSG). Who changed? Did Jesus change or the disciples? This Scripture should help you so much! Jesus is going to mature you so that you really understand what He is talking about and your heart has grown in love!

When people read the Bible to you or tell you spiritual things that are amazing to them, it doesn't always excite you as much as when you discover it yourself. It is like when you hear all about a new kid at school. It may make you interested in meeting him or her, but you are not about to become friends until you spend time with the kid yourself.

The more time Solomon spent with God, the wiser he became: "God gave Solomon wisdom—the deepest of understanding and the largest of hearts. There was nothing beyond him, nothing he couldn't handle. . . . Sent by kings from all over the earth who had heard of his reputation, people came from far and near to listen to the wisdom of Solomon" (I Kings 4:29-34). You aren't growing well spiritually until you discover God for yourself.

Teacher Notes

Student Question/Reflection

Sometimes we can get tired waiting for God to do what he's promised. What can you do to keep trusting him and doing what he wants you to do?

QUESTION/REFLECTION

Question/Reflection

Sometimes we can get tired waiting for God to do what he's promised. What can you do to keep trusting him and doing what he wants you to do?

WORKBOOK CHAPTER 6

💡 TIP FOR PARENTS:

It is always helpful to your children to help them see where they have grown in connecting to God. Try and remember something that was hard for them to understand that God was doing earlier in their life, something that they just get now, and share that with them. Maybe it was how to read the Bible (before they struggled and now it's natural), or maybe they had a hard time seeking God for direction but now they are able to do it easily. As a parent, when you affirm their growth in connecting to their spiritual life, it helps to build their spiritual identity.

Teaching Point 18

GOD IS ALWAYS TEACHING YOU AND SHARING HIMSELF WITH YOU

GOD IS ALWAYS TEACHING YOU AND SHARING HIMSELF WITH YOU

TEACHING POINT 18

1. Biblical Foundations 6.3:
"God is Our Teacher"
2. Student Key Verse: 1 Timothy 4:12
3. Teaching Content 18
4. Student Question: *What are some ways you could spend more time with God and grow your friendship with Him?*

6.3 BIBLICAL FOUNDATIONS: GOD IS OUR TEACHER

When you go to school, you learn from teachers who specialize in certain subjects. Jesus is our Master Teacher. He knows all things and wants to teach us. He always knows what is best, and He loves to bring us to a better place of understanding in every area of life. He is constantly sharing His life and knowledge with us. When we desire to be taught by Him, we will be so blessed in our life. "You address me as 'Teacher' and 'Master,' and rightly so. That is what I am" (John 13:13).

Student Key Verse

1 Timothy 4:12: "Don't let anyone put you down because you're young. Teach believers with your life: by word, by demeanor, by love, by faith, by integrity."

GOD IS ALWAYS TEACHING YOU AND SHARING HIMSELF WITH YOU

When you spend time with God, it's always good to see where God is in your relationships and life. You know you are growing up in God when you can see Him working in everything. Maybe you are reading a book and something good happens to the main character that makes you happy too. If you see that happening through God's eyes, He's showing you that you have His heart of love for others: "Laugh with your happy friends when they're happy; share tears when they're down" (Romans 12:14).

God is always teaching you and sharing Himself with you, but you need the Holy Spirit to see it. When God speaks to you, it helps you to understand even more of who He is and who you are. King David said that God was good to him even when he was going through valleys that he could get hurt in. David ended the psalm saying: "Your beauty and love chase after me every day of my life. I'm back home in the house of God for the rest of my life" (Psalm 23:6). When you stop and reflect on what God's doing in your life and ask Him what He wants to show you, you give Him an opportunity to love on you and teach you more.

When you read the Bible and understand how you can apply what you read to your own life, it means you are maturing in your relationship with God. Don't get discouraged if you don't see a lot happening. Just like growing up is a process, so is growing up with God! Paul told Timothy "Don't let anyone put you down because you're young" (1 Timothy 4:12 MSG). Any person, no matter how young or old, can have an amazing relationship with God.

Teacher Notes

_____

_____

_____

_____

_____

_____

_____

_____

_____

_____

_____

_____

_____

_____

_____

_____

_____

Student Question/Reflection

What are some ways you could spend more time with God and grow your friendship with him?

QUESTION/REFLECTION

Question/Reflection

What are some ways you could spend more time with God and grow your friendship with him?

WORKBOOK CHAPTER 6 115

_____

_____

TIP FOR PARENTS:

Talking to your kids about their spiritual development isn't always the easiest thing at first, but all kids like to see how they have grown. Think about how much our kids want to be measured to see if they even grew a centimeter! When you talk to your child about what God is growing them in, and you help them see areas in which they have grown, they will begin to see you, other family members, and friends the same way they look at those rulers—they will see their growth in your eyes.

My friend's son lied a lot. One day, he was caught lying at school, and when his dad talked to him, he admitted everything. His dad said, "Let's pray and ask God to show us why you are lying." And they did just that. His son said, "I do it because I never feel like I get what I want." So his dad said, "That's hard that you feel that way, but that's a bad reason to lie. Do you want to give that to God and ask Him to help change you and see when you are getting what He wants you to have?" His son agreed. After a few weeks, he saw a dramatic change in his son. He asked him, "How are you doing with what we prayed about a few weeks back?" His son said: "Dad, I feel like things have turned around. It's like God is showing me every time I get what I am desiring or praying for, unless I am not supposed to have it! I don't feel like I even want to lie or that I need to!" It was a profound moment for them both. His dad was so proud.

Your kids are processing complex emotions and navigating their spiritual journey each day, and each time they are connecting to people and learning more. Being a source of connection for them starts with simple conversations. Ask questions like:

What are you growing character-wise?

What do you think God is doing in your heart right now?

What do you love that God is doing in your life?

What has been a challenge in growing in God right now?

ACTIVATION

INDIVIDUAL ACTIVITY AND INSTRUCTION

Can you remember something that God showed you that perhaps you didn't understand? Maybe it was a dream or a vision, or maybe it was a parable in the Bible you still want to understand. Take the next five minutes to ask God again what He meant by it. Sometimes when He talks to you, it sounds just like your own thoughts. You can tell it's Him talking because it sounds kind and it's something He would want to tell just you, not everyone else.

_____

_____

_____

_____

_____

_____

_____

_____

_____

_____

_____

_____

_____

_____

ACTIVATION, CONTINUED...

GROUP ACTIVITY AND INSTRUCTION

Everyone in the group: Think about one of the hard times you have been through and what God taught you through it. Take two minutes each to share the hard thing in one sentence. For example: "I broke my ankle and couldn't play soccer for a season." "We had to move because of my dad's new job." "I was bullied at school." "I went on a mission trip and saw a lot of poor children." Then after you share that one sentence, share what God taught you and how He grew you closer to Him through it. Congratulations, now you are all teachers!

GROWTH PRAYER

God, help me to obey You when You ask me to do things even when it is hard sometimes. Help me to know when You do something in me and through me because I want to see Your presence and Your love at work in my life. Thank You for sharing Yourself with me. Thank You for teaching me daily how to be like You and how to live an awesome life.

Amen!

ACTIVATION PAGE
I WILL SEE PEOPLE AS IF THEY'VE ALREADY WON AT LIFE

On the trophy, write the names of three people that you are called to see in fullness at the end of their lives, as if they have already won the trophy for living out their purpose well. Tell God you are willing to see them this way, and then write something you see about them that maybe they haven't accomplished yet, but that you will believe for. For example: "She will go to college to get a master's degree." "He will make a lot of money in business." "He will be a great athlete."

Scripture: With both feet planted firmly on love, you'll be able to take in with all followers of Jesus the extravagant dimensions of Christ's love. Reach out and experience the breadth! Test its length! Plumb the depths! Rise to the heights! Live full lives, full in the fullness of God.
- Ephesians 3:14-19

PRINTABLE ACTIVATION PAGE AVAILABLE IN TEACHER REPRODUCIBLE PAGES - PAGE 241

PRINTABLE COLORING PAGE AVAILABLE IN TEACHER REPRODUCIBLE PAGES - PAGE 241

CHAPTER 7 CHECKLIST

- ☐ Read Chapter 7 in *Growing Up with God*
- ☐ Choose DVD – Option One or Two
- ☐ Read aloud: Student testimonials
- ☐ Review with Students: Synopsis

TEACHING POINT 19:
YOUR GOAL IS TO LOVE

- ☐ Teach / Review Biblical Foundations
  Biblical Foundations 7.1:
  "Love Is The Only Way"
- ☐ Share: Student Key Verse
  Philippians 2:2
- ☐ Teach / Review: Teaching Content 19
  Your goal is to love
- ☐ Student Question / Reflection
  Have you ever stopped doing something for yourself and focused on helping someone else instead? How did that feel?

TEACHING POINT 20:
TAKE RISKS WITH WHAT YOU HEAR FROM GOD

- ☐ Teach / Review Biblical Foundations
  Biblical Foundations 7.2:
  "Taking Risk Is Important"
- ☐ Share: Student Key Verse
  Hebrews 4:12
- ☐ Teach / Review: Teaching Content 20
  Take risks with what you hear from God
- ☐ Student Question / Reflection
  Have you ever obeyed what you thought Jesus was saying to do even though it was hard? What happened?

TEACHING POINT 21:
WHEN YOU OBEY GOD AND WALK WITH HIM, YOU CAN'T HELP BUT FEEL HIS FRIENDSHIP

- ☐ Teach / Review Biblical Foundations
  Biblical Foundations 7.3:
  "Trust Brings Adventure"
- ☐ Share: Student Key Verse
  Ephesians 1:17
- ☐ Teach / Review: Teaching Content 21
  When you obey God and walk with Him, you can't help but feel His friendship
- ☐ Student Question / Reflection
  How has God done good things in your heart and life after hard times or pain?

PRAY GROWTH PRAYER

GROWTH ACTIVITIES

- ☐ Individual
- ☐ Group
- ☐ Activity Page
- ☐ Coloring Page
- ☐ Implement parenting tip into weekly life

Growing Up with God

CHAPTER

7

TEACHER GUIDE - CHAPTER 7 OVERVIEW

CHAPTER 7 OVERVIEW

- ☐ Teaching Overview
- ☐ Chapter Synopsis
- ☐ DVD Session 7
- ☐ Growth Prayer

TEACHING POINT 19:
YOUR GOAL IS TO LOVE

1. Biblical Foundations 7.1:

"Love Is The Only Way"

2. Student Key Verse: Philippians 2:2

3. Teaching Content 19

4. Student Question: *Have you ever stopped doing something for yourself and focused on helping someone else instead? How did that feel?*

TEACHING POINT 21:
WHEN YOU OBEY GOD AND WALK WITH HIM, YOU CAN'T HELP BUT FEEL HIS FRIENDSHIP

1. Biblical Foundations 7.3:

"Trust Brings Adventure"

2. Student Key Verse: Ephesians 1:17-18

3. Teaching Content 21

4. Student Question: *How has God done good things in your heart and life after hard times or pain?*

TEACHING POINT 20:
TAKE RISKS WITH WHAT YOU HEAR FROM GOD

1. Biblical Foundations 7.2:

"Taking Risks is Important"

2. Student Key Verse: Hebrews 4:12-13

3. Teaching Content 20

4. Student Question: *Have you ever obeyed what you thought Jesus was saying to do even though it was hard? What happened?*

GROWTH ACTIVITIES

1. Individual
2. Group
3. Activity Page
4. Coloring Page
5. Growth Prayer

STORY SYNOPSIS

Maria wants the main role in the musical more than anything she's ever wanted in her whole life. When she hears that Lucas's grandmother sold her house, it gives her even more faith that God is going to help her as well.

Brooke is sick when she comes to audition and can't sing. At first, Maria is happy because now she'll get the main role. Then she remembers what God showed her: loving people like Brooke is her destiny. She feels that loving Brooke is more important than getting the role, so she and Hartley walk over to Brooke and pray that she will be healed. Brooke is healed and gets the main part, but Maria doesn't care because she's done what God asked her to do. For the first time in her relationship with God, she understands what being a friend of God feels like.

CHILD'S TESTIMONY

Mordekai's Testimony, Age 8

One Friday night we went on a treasure hunt. Before we went out, we asked God who was on His heart and where He wanted us to go. I heard God tell me that we should go to Wal-Mart. I saw a map of where in Wal-Mart we needed to go, which was by the fish tanks.

We found a woman in that exact spot, and when we told her why we were there, she starting crying. She was sad because her kid was going to go live with his dad instead of her. She felt like God didn't care about how bad that felt. We told her how God did care a lot—He showed us exactly where she would be standing and what she would be wearing. We were able to tell her about Jesus and about how much God loved her. She felt a lot happier after we prayed with her. The whole church was excited about what happened.

LET'S GET STARTED

Let's jump right into Chapter 7! If you have elected to have your students read each chapter as they go along with the DVDs, then now is the time to read Chapter 7 in *Growing Up with God*. If your students are reading their book outside of your class setting, then please skip down to the teaching points.

PLAY DVD SESSION 7

OPTION 1:

Watch entire Session seven and go back and review all three Teaching Points together.

OPTION 2:

1. Watch the Chapter seven synopsis, Shawn's engaging story, and Teaching Point nineteen.
2. Pause the DVD for Student Question/ Reflection activity.
3. Resume DVD for Teaching Point twenty.
4. Pause the DVD for Student Question/ Reflection activity.
5. Resume DVD for Teaching Point twenty-one.
6. Pause the DVD for Student Question/ Reflection activity.

GROWTH PRAYER
PRAY ALONG WITH SHAWN ON THE DVD GROWTH PRAYER

God, help my goal in life be to love—to love You, myself, and the world around me! Help me to take risks to love people and hear Your heart. Thank You that when I obey what You tell me to do, I can feel Your friendship. Help me to see what Your will is and who I am supposed to love!

Amen!

Let's keep growing!

Teacher Notes:

_____

_____

_____

_____

_____

_____

_____

_____

Teaching Point 19
YOUR GOAL IS TO LOVE

Page 124

YOUR GOAL IS TO LOVE

TEACHING POINT 19

1. Biblical Foundations 7.1:
"Love Is The Only Way"
2. Student Key Verse: Philippians 2:2
3. Teaching Content 19
4. Student Question: *Have you ever stopped doing something for yourself and focused on helping someone else instead? How did that feel?*

7.1 BIBLICAL FOUNDATIONS: LOVE IS THE ONLY WAY

In all things, we should have love as the only goal. If love is not your ultimate goal, then you will always feel like you are not having a full life. The kingdom of heaven is made up of three things: faith, hope, and love, but the greatest of these is love. Love gives us life and the capacity to do things. Love is perfect, and if we partner with love, we will do our best! God is love, and if we are not loving, then we are not serving God! "I tell you, love your enemies. Help and give without expecting a return. You'll never—I promise—regret it. Live out this God-created identity the way our Father lives toward us, generously and graciously, even when we're at our worst. Our Father is kind; you be kind" (Luke 6:35–36).

Student Key Verse

Philippians 2:2: "Agree with each other, love each other, be deep-spirited friends."

YOUR GOAL IS TO LOVE

There will always be a temptation to do better or outperform others, but that is not the goal of a Christian. Your goal is to love like Jesus, and sometimes that means putting other people's needs before your own.

"If you've gotten anything at all out of following Christ, if his love has made any difference in your life, if being in a community of the Spirit means anything to you, if you have a heart, if you care— then do me a favor: Agree with each other, love each other, be deep-spirited friends. Don't push your way to the front; don't sweet-talk your way to the top. Put yourself aside, and help others get ahead. Don't be obsessed with getting your own advantage. Forget yourselves long enough to lend a helping hand" (Philippians 2:1-4).

Maria could have been the star of the show, but she would have missed out on a friendship with Brooke for the sake of accomplishing her dream. Sometimes you can be so focused on yourself and achieving your goals that you forget to include the #1 goal—to love others! Can you imagine what sports would look like if we were still trying to win but cared about the other players as much as the game we were playing? It would change the atmosphere of sports!

Only people who are growing up in God trust God enough to know that He cares about their dreams more than they do. You don't have to feel like it's only up to you to make things happen. God will do so much on your behalf, more than you could hope for or imagine (see Ephesians 3:20). You can feel peaceful about being happy to help others succeed and put their needs in front of your own. People without a relationship with God don't have this assurance that God will do amazing things for them, but we know God will come through for us. And when you know God is doing good things for you, you can give away positions and rewards. The way God's love works, the more you give away, the more you get from God!

Student
Question/Reflection

If you were going to love like Jesus, what would be different in your life?

Have you ever stopped doing something for yourself and focused on helping someone else instead? How did that feel?

_____

_____

_____

_____

_____

_____

_____

QUESTION/REFLECTION

Question/Reflection

Have you ever stopped doing something for yourself and focused on helping someone else instead? How did that feel?

_____

_____

_____

_____

_____

_____

_____

WORKBOOK CHAPTER 7 127

_____

_____

_____

_____

_____

_____

_____

_____

_____

_____

Teaching Point 20
TAKE RISKS WITH WHAT YOU HEAR FROM GOD

Page 127-128

TAKE RISKS WITH WHAT YOU HEAR FROM GOD

TEACHING POINT 20

1. Biblical Foundations 7.2:
"Taking Risks is Important"
2. Student Key Verse: Hebrews 4:12-13
3. Teaching Content 20
4. Student Question: *Have you ever obeyed what you thought Jesus was saying to do, even though it was hard? What happened?*

7.2 BIBLICAL FOUNDATIONS: TAKING RISKS IS IMPORTANT

It is not always easy to step out of your comfort zone and do something God wants you to do. Peter and John (in the Bible) were at the gate called Beautiful, and God pointed someone out to them. They felt God wanted them to stop what they were doing to help him. It must have been challenging to take that kind of risk. They recognized the person they were stopping for, but they didn't know him; he was a stranger. The Bible says they fixed their eyes on him. They didn't even have any money to offer him, which is what he was asking for. But they knew he could be healed because they saw Jesus heal so many people, and they had moved in healing before. Peter and John prayed for him and he was healed! Step out and take risk with what God tells you. "When he saw Peter and John about to enter the Temple, he asked for a handout. Peter, with John at his side, looked him straight in the eye and said, 'Look here.' He looked up, expecting to get something from them. Peter said, 'I don't have a nickel to my name, but what I do have, I give you: In the name of Jesus Christ of Nazareth, walk!' He grabbed him by the right hand and pulled him up. In an instant his feet and ankles became firm. He jumped to his feet and walked" (Acts 3:3–8).

Student Key Verse

Hebrews 4:12: "God means what he says. What he says goes."

TAKE RISKS WITH WHAT YOU HEAR FROM GOD

There are times to take risks with your faith that aren't always convenient. It is worth taking a risk as a Christian to do something you think God has asked you to do. The worst that could happen is that nothing gets better, or your friends make fun of you. Think about this, though. Because your goal is love, people can have the opportunity to feel loved and connected to God through your obedience.

This is why it's so important to know what God is saying to you so you can go and do it straightaway. God always has really good reasons for asking us to obey. Sometimes we won't understand why He wants us to do or say things until we see the end result. We can trust Him. "God means what he says. What he says goes. His powerful Word is sharp as a surgeon's scalpel, cutting through everything, whether doubt or defense, laying us open to listen and obey. Nothing and no one is impervious (resistant) to God's Word. We can't get away from it—no matter what" (Hebrews 4:12-13).

Maria had to risk her opportunity to get the main role in the play by praying for Brooke. Brooke or her mom might have been mad at Maria's desire to bring a religious moment into a show choir. The director or other teacher's might have judged Maria for praying for Brooke. Maria had pure motives though. She wanted to see God move, and when she put her own wishes to one side and reached out to Brooke with God's love, she saw God come.

Sometimes you can get in trouble for wanting to see God show up in your everyday life. There are people who will get mad at you for trying, but if your motive is love, it never fails. Jesus even tells people that they are blessed or favored whenever people misunderstand them for the sake of their faith. When you walk with God in His love, or obey God, you can't help but feel His friendship. Love always wins!

Teacher Notes

_____

_____

_____

_____

_____

_____

_____

_____

_____

_____

_____

_____

_____

_____

_____

_____

_____

_____

Student Question/Reflection

Have you ever obeyed what you thought Jesus was saying to do, even though it was hard? What happened?

Question/Reflection

Have you ever obeyed what you thought Jesus was saying to do, even though it was hard? What happened?

WORKBOOK CHAPTER 7

TIP FOR PARENTS:

This part of the story (Maria praying for another competitor) came from a real experience of a ten-year-old who wanted to pray for another actor in a secular audition for a TV show. His mom actually did a great job of outlining the risk, but she encouraged him to make a decision based on his heart and faith. Sometimes our kids feel afraid to do something, but they don't even know why or what they are processing in that fear. Helping them articulate what they are afraid of is so powerful, because then they know what they are battling.

A little girl in our church was going to sing in a choir performance and then realized she didn't want to, when it was time, because it felt scary. Her mom asked her, "What do you think you are afraid of?" She said, like most kids, "I don't know. I just don't want to do it anymore." Her mom said, "Tell me three things that you think you are most afraid of." She thought about it and said, "That people will laugh at me. That I don't have a good voice. That I will forget the words." This was great, because now the mom had something to work with. She prayed and asked God for wisdom and then said to her daughter, "Have you ever seen anyone get laughed at at a choir performance before?" Her daughter hadn't and grew a little more secure. "Yeah, that's not going to happen," her mom said. Then she asked, "Did your teacher give any parts to people who have awful voices?" Her daughter knew he hadn't, so that one was going now, too. "Do you remember the words now to the song?" Her daughter nodded her head. "Well, the odds are that you won't forget them in the next half hour. Why don't you try?" Her daughter, having faced her fears and given them language, felt more confident now to try. Then her mom asked, "Why do you want to sing?" Her daughter said, "Because I like to. And because music is beautiful." Her mom said, "Don't you think your desire for singing and your love for the beauty of music should be more powerful than your fear about it?" This made sense to her and she was ready to choose it! She gave a beautiful performance and remembered all the words.

Teaching Point 21

WHEN YOU OBEY GOD AND WALK WITH HIM, YOU CAN'T HELP BUT FEEL HIS FRIENDSHIP

WHEN YOU OBEY GOD AND WALK WITH HIM, YOU CAN'T HELP BUT FEEL HIS FRIENDSHIP

TEACHING POINT 21

1. Biblical Foundations 7.3:
"Trust Brings Adventure"
2. Student Key Verse: Ephesians 1:17
3. Teaching Content 21
4. Student Question: *How has God done good things in your heart and life after hard times or pain?*

7.3 BIBLICAL FOUNDATIONS: TRUST BRINGS ADVENTURE

Connecting with God starts with trust. "Trust" is having a firm belief in the reliability, truth, ability, or strength of someone or something. When we start to trust God, we open our heart and life to His amazing possibilities. There is a king talked about in Scripture who trusted God more than any other king in his day. His name was Hezekiah. Hezekiah put his whole trust in God. Not 10 percent, not 50 percent, but he put 100 percent of his trust in God! Wow! God rewarded Hezekiah with a deep connection to Him throughout all of his adventures. "Hezekiah put his whole trust in the God of Israel. There was no king quite like him, either before or after. He held fast to God—never loosened his grip—and obeyed to the letter everything God had commanded Moses. And God, for his part, held fast to him through all his adventures" (2 Kings 18:5–6).

Student Key Verse

Ephesians 1:17: "When I heard of the solid trust you have in the Master Jesus and your outpouring of love to all the followers of Jesus, I couldn't stop thanking God for you."

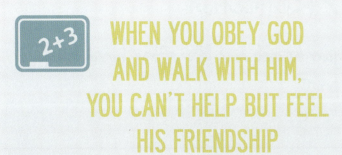

WHEN YOU OBEY GOD AND WALK WITH HIM, YOU CAN'T HELP BUT FEEL HIS FRIENDSHIP

Jesus said to the disciples that obedience is even better than service. When you learn how to follow Him as a friend, then you truly know Him. Paul knew this. He said to his friends: "You're looking at this backward. The issue in Jerusalem is not what they do to me . . . but what the Master Jesus does through my obedience. Can't you see that?" (Acts 21:13) He knew how good God was and trusted Him completely.

Jesus wants us to know everything about Him at a heart-to-heart level! Paul even prayed over the Ephesians: "I ask—ask the God of our Master, Jesus Christ, the God of glory—to make you intelligent and discerning in knowing him personally, your eyes focused and clear, so that you can see exactly what it is he is calling you to do, grasp the immensity of this glorious way of life he has for his followers, oh, the utter extravagance of his work in us who trust him—endless energy, boundless strength! (Ephesians 1:17-18) Doing life with Jesus is glorious! When you know Him personally and trust Him, He gives you boundless energy and strength!

Even when hard things happen, friends of God know that God will find a way to bring good things out of the difficult times. People who aren't friends with God don't have that promise, so it's harder for them to take big risks that may not pay off. Failure to them means loss. For you, even when you lose, God works it out for your gain!

Teacher Notes

_____

_____

_____

_____

_____

_____

_____

_____

_____

_____

_____

_____

_____

_____

Student
Question/Reflection

How has God done good things in your heart and life after hard times or pain?

_____

_____

_____

_____

_____

_____

_____

_____

QUESTION/REFLECTION

Question/Reflection

How has God done good things in your heart and life after hard times or pain?

_____

_____

WORKBOOK CHAPTER 7 135

_____

_____

_____

_____

_____

_____

ACTIVATION

INDIVIDUAL ACTIVITY AND INSTRUCTION

Increase your conversation with God by talking to Him for a minute or two seven times a day for seven days. When you wake up, talk to God as if He's your best friend (because He is). Tell Him about what you are going to do that day and that you're happy He'll be with you while you do it all. Talk to Him before you sit down to eat, or when you get done with school or church. Talk to Him about your relationships and life. Right before you go to bed, tell God about what you loved throughout the day and see if there was any way you loved like Jesus. Ask Him to help you grow.

_____

_____

_____

_____

_____

_____

_____

_____

_____

_____

_____

_____

ACTIVATION, CONTINUED...

GROUP ACTIVITY AND INSTRUCTION

Pray together and ask God for a risk you could take in sharing something from His heart—for someone in your life who doesn't know Him. Maybe you could write a card or a letter to a relative, or you could call a friend. Maybe invite someone over you don't know well and share your faith with him or her. Maybe pray for someone who is having a hard time. Make a plan and write it down. Next time you get together, report what happened! If nothing happened and all that you did was make a plan, congrats anyway—you are learning how to include other people you wouldn't normally hang out with.

_____

_____

_____

_____

_____

_____

_____

_____

_____

_____

GROWTH PRAYER

God, help my goal in life be to love--to love You, myself, and the world around me! Help me to take risks to love people and hear Your heart. Thank You that when I obey what You tell me to do, I can feel Your friendship. Help me to see what Your will is and who I am supposed to love!

Amen!

Let's keep growing!

ACTIVATION PAGE
I WILL TAKE SPIRITUAL RISKS!

It is worth taking a risk as a Christian to do something you think God has asked you to do. The worst that could happen is that nothing gets better, or your friends make fun of you. Under Jesus's foot/in the water, draw or write something that would be a big spiritual risk for you to take. Now pray God gives you the opportunity to take it!

Scripture: I ask—ask the God of our Master, Jesus Christ, the God of glory—to make you intelligent and discerning in knowing him personally, your eyes focused and clear, so that you can see exactly what it is he is calling you to do, grasp the immensity of this glorious way of life he has for his followers. — Ephesians 1:17-18

PRINTABLE ACTIVATION PAGE AVAILABLE IN TEACHER REPRODUCIBLE PAGES - PAGE 241

PRINTABLE COLORING PAGE AVAILABLE IN TEACHER REPRODUCIBLE PAGES - PAGE 241

CHAPTER 8 CHECKLIST

- ☐ Read Chapter 8 in *Growing Up with God*
- ☐ Choose DVD – Option One or Two
- ☐ Read aloud: Student testimonials
- ☐ Review with Students: Synopsis

TEACHING POINT 22:
YOUR FRIENDSHIP WITH GOD EVEN HELPS THOSE WHO DON'T KNOW HIM!

- ☐ Teach / Review Biblical Foundations
  Biblical Foundations 8.1:
  "Your Relationship Changes Everything"
- ☐ Share: Student Key Verse
  Galatians 6:4
- ☐ Teach / Review: Teaching Content 22
  Your friendship with God even helps those who don't know Him
- ☐ Student Question / Reflection
  How has God's love from other people helped your heart? Can you imagine how other people's hearts could fill up on His love when you love them like Jesus, even if they don't know Him?

TEACHING POINT 23:
YOU CAN BLESS OTHERS BY GIVING AWAY WHAT GOD HAS GIVEN YOU

- ☐ Teach / Review Biblical Foundations
  Biblical Foundations 8.2:
  "Generosity Is Contagious"
- ☐ Share: Student Key Verse
  Matthew 18:20
- ☐ Teach / Review: Teaching Content 23
  You can bless others by giving away what God has given you
- ☐ Student Question / Reflection
  If you think about the ideas and thoughts you've already come up with in your times with God, which ones do you know were ideas

TEACHING POINT 23: CONTINUED...
YOU CAN BLESS OTHERS BY GIVING AWAY WHAT GOD HAS GIVEN YOU

and thoughts given to you by God? Can you see how God could use some of them to help make other people's lives better?

TEACHING POINT 24:
GOD BRINGS SOMETHING GOOD OUT OF EVERYTHING

- ☐ Teach / Review Biblical Foundations
  Biblical Foundations 8.3:
  "God Is Good"
- ☐ Share: Student Key Verse
  Romans 8:28
- ☐ Teach / Review: Teaching Content 24
  God brings something good out of everything
- ☐ Student Question / Reflection
  Can you see where God has brought something good out of some of the sad things that have happened in your life?

PRAY GROWTH PRAYER

GROWTH ACTIVITIES

- ☐ Individual
- ☐ Group
- ☐ Activity Page
- ☐ Coloring Page
- ☐ Implement parenting tip into weekly life

Growing Up with God
CHAPTER
8

TEACHER GUIDE - CHAPTER 8 OVERVIEW

CHAPTER 8 OVERVIEW

☐ Teaching Overview   ☐ DVD Session 8

☐ Chapter Synopsis   ☐ Growth Prayer

TEACHING POINT 22:
YOUR FRIENDSHIP WITH GOD EVEN HELPS THOSE WHO DON'T KNOW HIM

1. Biblical Foundations 8.1:

"Your Relationship Changes Everything"

2. Student Key Verse: Galations 6:4

3. Teaching Content 22

4. Student Question: *How has God's love from other people helped your heart? Can you imagine how other people's hearts could fill up on His love when you love them like Jesus, even if they don't know Him?*

TEACHING POINT 24:
GOD BRINGS SOMETHING GOOD OUT OF EVERYTHING

1. Biblical Foundations 8.3:

"God Is Good"

2. Student Key Verse: Romans 8:28

3. Teaching Content 24

4. Student Question: *Can you see where God has brought something good out of some of the sad things that have happened in your life?*

TEACHING POINT 23:
YOU CAN BLESS OTHERS BY GIVING AWAY WHAT GOD HAS GIVEN YOU

1. Biblical Foundations 8.2:

"Generosity is Contagious"

2. Student Key Verse: Matthew 18:20

3. Teaching Content 23

4. Student Question: *If you think about the ideas and thoughts you've already come up with in your times with God, which ones do you know were ideas and thoughts given to you by God? Can you see how God could use some of them to make other people's lives better?*

GROWTH ACTIVITIES

1. Individual
2. Group
3. Activity Page
4. Coloring Page
5. Growth Prayer

STORY SYNOPSIS

Jeffrey, the bully, begins to pick on the friends after school one day. Lucas prays for help and hears the Holy Spirit tell him to talk to Jeffrey one-on-one, on behalf of Jamal. God shows Lucas his heart for Jeffrey. Lucas feels that perhaps Jeffrey is going through some of the same problems at home that Jamal is. Lucas is filled with compassion for Jeffrey, which helps Lucas show Jeffrey that he cares about his pain. He appeals to Jeffrey and tells him that God doesn't want Jeffrey's life to be hard, that He loves him, and that He can help him. He also asks him to leave Jamal alone. Jeffrey agrees to back down.

That night, Lucas's parents share that they have been praying about adopting another boy, and ask Lucas if he would consider welcoming Jamal into their family. He shares his word with them from last year's summer camp about being a brother.

CHILD'S TESTIMONY

D'Shawn's Testimony, Age 8

I was praying in my room and heard God tell me that my daddy would be home for Christmas. He was away with the army in another country called Afghanistan. My mom didn't know if she could believe me, and she told me Daddy wasn't supposed to come back until the next summer. Then, after Thanksgiving, my daddy surprised us by coming home early, and he got us good! His whole troop got to come home for Christmas and he doesn't have to go away from us again. I was able to tell my daddy that Jesus told me he was coming home for a Christmas present.

LET'S GET STARTED

Let's jump right into Chapter 8! If you have elected to have your students read each chapter as they go along with the DVDs, then now is the time to read Chapter 8 in *Growing Up with God*. If your students are reading their book outside of your class setting, then please skip down to the teaching points.

PLAY DVD SESSION 8

OPTION 1:

Watch entire Session eight and go back and review all three Teaching Points together.

OPTION 2:

1. Watch the Chapter eight synopsis, Shawn's engaging story, and Teaching Point twenty-two.
2. Pause the DVD for Student Question/Reflection activity.
3. Resume DVD for Teaching Point twenty-three.
4. Pause the DVD for Student Question/Reflection activity.
5. Resume DVD for Teaching Point twenty-four.
6. Pause the DVD for Student Question/Reflection activity.

GROWTH PRAYER
PRAY ALONG WITH SHAWN ON THE DVD GROWTH PRAYER

God, I pray that my friendship with You will help people who don't even know You connect to You. Help me share what You are doing in my heart to others. Help me to trust that You will bring good things out of everything in my life, even when it is hard. Show me how to see things through Your eyes so I can see what You are doing and stay encouraged and hopeful.

Amen!

It's time to grow!

Teacher Notes:

_____

_____

_____

_____

_____

_____

_____

_____

Teaching Point 22

YOUR FRIENDSHIP WITH GOD EVEN HELPS THOSE WHO DON'T KNOW HIM

YOUR FRIENDSHIP WITH GOD EVEN HELPS THOSE WHO DON'T KNOW HIM

TEACHING POINT 22

1. Biblical Foundations 8.1:
"Your Relationship Changes Everything"
2. Student Key Verse: Galations 6:4
3. Teaching Content 22
4. Student Question: *How has God's love from other people helped your heart? Can you imagine how other people's hearts could fill up on His love when you love them like Jesus, even if they don't know Him?*

8.1 BIBLICAL FOUNDATIONS: YOUR RELATIONSHIP CHANGES EVERYTHING

Joseph (in the Bible) loved the Lord and served Him wherever he was. At one point in Joseph's life he was a prisoner to Pharaoh. That didn't stop Joseph from loving God and doing what was right. His relationship with God never skipped one beat. Pharaoh had a dream one night and the only person who could interpret the dream was Joseph. Joseph was able to help Pharaoh and eventually the entire country because of Joseph's faithfulness to God. Your relationship with God changes things even though you may not see it. "So Pharaoh commissioned Joseph: 'I'm putting you in charge of the entire country of Egypt.' Then Pharaoh removed his signet ring from his finger and slipped it on Joseph's hand. He outfitted him in robes of the best linen and put a gold chain around his neck. He put the second-in-command chariot at his disposal, and as he rode people shouted 'Bravo!' Joseph was in charge of the entire country of Egypt. Pharaoh told Joseph, 'I am Pharaoh, but no one in Egypt will make a single move without your stamp of approval'" (Genesis 41:41–44).

Student Key Verse

Galatians 6:4: "Make a careful exploration of who you are and the work you have been given, and then sink yourself into that."

YOUR FRIENDSHIP WITH GOD EVEN HELPS THOSE WHO DON'T KNOW HIM

As Lucas invested time and friendship in Jamal, Jamal became more confident, very focused, and a great contributor to their friendship group. Your friendship with God will even help people who don't know Him behave differently. Your friendship with God and your character that God grows in you actually helps people around you grow as well.

"Use your heads as you live and work among outsiders. Don't miss a trick. Make the most of every opportunity. Be gracious in your speech. The goal is to bring out the best in others in a conversation, not put them down, not cut them out" (Colossians 4:5-6). When you include others and let them know that you see good things in them, they can feel the love of God filling up their hearts.

In other words, your life gives others opportunities to know what God is like because the more time you spend with God, the more you start to act like Him. God is doing things in you that affect the world around you in great ways. You get to bring out the best in others around you when you love them like God does. Your goals for your life are different. When you put the love in your heart into conversations and daily activities, you change the atmosphere around you. That atmosphere of love changes people's lives.

"We have three things to do: ...Trust steadily in God, hope unswervingly, love extravagantly. And the best of the three is love" (I Corinthians 13:13). "I tell you, love your enemies. Help and give without expecting a return. You'll never—I promise—regret it. Live out this God-created identity the way our Father lives toward us, generously and graciously, even when we're at our worst. Our Father is kind; you be kind" (Luke 6:35-36).

Teacher Notes

Student Question/Reflection

How has God's love from other people helped your heart? Can you imagine how other people's hearts could fill up on his love when you love them like Jesus, even if they don't know him?

QUESTION/REFLECTION

Question/Reflection

How has God's love from other people helped your heart? Can you imagine how other people's hearts could fill up on his love when you love them like Jesus, even if they don't know him?

WORKBOOK CHAPTER 8 147

_____

_____

_____

_____

_____

_____

_____

_____

_____

_____

_____

 TIP FOR PARENTS:

It is great to get your kids in a volunteer role in their school or for extra-curricular activities. It not only prepares them for leadership but also helps them set a foundation to influence with their lives and their faith. Serving and acts of service help your children to be influencers and help them to learn to connect to others in a positive way.

Teaching Point 23

YOU CAN BLESS OTHERS BY GIVING AWAY WHAT GOD HAS GIVEN YOU

YOU CAN BLESS OTHERS BY GIVING AWAY WHAT GOD HAS GIVEN YOU

TEACHING POINT 23

1. Biblical Foundations 8.2:
"Generosity is Contagious"
2. Student Key Verse: Matthew 18:20
3. Teaching Content 23
4. Student Question: *If you think about the ideas and thoughts you've already come up with in your times with God, which ones do you know were ideas and thoughts given to you by God? Can you see how God could use some of them to make other people's lives better?*

8.2 BIBLICAL FOUNDATIONS: GENEROSITY IS CONTAGIOUS

God desires to be so generous toward you that it would blow your mind. He wants you to be so full of His kingdom that you can't help but give it away. When God blesses you, He is setting you up to bless those around you. By wonderful design, all of the world speaks of His works and praises Him for it. Each and every time you are blessed by God, it should remind you to be a blessing to others because you have been treated so generously. "You have been treated generously, so live generously" (Matthew 10:8).

Student Key Verse

Matthew 18:20: "When two or three of you are together because of me, you can be sure that I'll be there."

YOU CAN BLESS OTHERS BY GIVING AWAY WHAT GOD HAS GIVEN YOU

The word "impart" means to spiritually give away or reproduce—like making a copy of a picture on a copy machine. The compassion Lucas felt for Jamal and Jeffrey was given to him by God. He was able to appeal to Jeffrey in a way that made Jeffrey feel like Lucas understood what he was going through, which is what God's love can feel like sometimes. When Lucas shared about Jamal's situation, Jeffrey believed him because Lucas was speaking with compassion instead of anger.

You can communicate the things God is doing in you and showing you. You can share the Holy Spirit in you with Christians when you pray for them and give away what God has given you. You can bless the world around you with your ideas, thoughts, beliefs, love culture, and more. Jesus was constantly imparting His ideas to the crowds who gathered around Him—ideas of what heaven was like, what God was like, and what life should be like. "When two of you get together on anything at all on earth and make a prayer of it, my Father in heaven goes into action. And when two or three of you are together because of me, you can be sure that I'll be there" (Matthew 18:19-20).

Jesus showed people that God wasn't a huge mean God who was mad at people and was always judging them. He showed everyone that God is a loving kind Father who cares a lot about everyone's interests.

When God shows you something, it is never just for you, although you might be the main one impacted by what you see. He does something for you so that He can do something through you that can affect your family, friends, and life. For Lucas, that meant that the "brothers" promise he was pursuing with Jamal was actually an answer to his parents' prayers to have another son. Their hearts opened to Jamal because of Lucas's deliberate friendship Him.

Teacher Notes

_____

_____

_____

_____

_____

_____

_____

_____

_____

_____

_____

_____

_____

_____

_____

_____

_____

_____

Student
Question/Reflection

If you think about the ideas and thoughts you've already come up with in your times with God, which ones do you know were ideas and thoughts given to you by God? Can you see how God could use some of them to help make other people's lives better?

_____

_____

_____

_____

_____

_____

_____

QUESTION/REFLECTION

Question/Reflection

If you think about the ideas and thoughts you've already come up with in your times with God, which ones do you know were ideas and thoughts given to you by God? Can you see how God could use some of them to help make other people's lives better?

_____

_____

WORKBOOK CHAPTER 8   151

_____

_____

_____

_____

_____

_____

_____

_____

Teaching Point 24

GOD BRINGS SOMETHING GOOD OUT OF EVERYTHING

GOD BRINGS SOMETHING GOOD OUT OF EVERYTHING

TEACHING POINT 24

1. Biblical Foundations 8.3:
"God Is Good"
2. Student Key Verse: Romans 8:28
3. Teaching Content 24
4. Student Question: *Can you see where God has brought something good out of some of the sad things that have happened in your life?*

8.3 BIBLICAL FOUNDATIONS: GOD IS GOOD

No matter the situation or circumstance, God remains the same. He is, and will always be, the Redeemer. He can't stop doing good; it is in His nature. When a child of God is careless in his walk, God is there to make things better. When a believer is excited about his faith journey, God makes his path straight and fills it with wonderful surprises. He is always making sure that we succeed, because we are His children. "I know how great this makes you feel, even though you have to put up with every kind of aggravation in the meantime. Pure gold put in the fire comes out of it proved pure; genuine faith put through this suffering comes out proved genuine. When Jesus wraps this all up, it's your faith, not your gold, that God will have on display as evidence of his victory" (1 Peter 1:6–7).

Student Key Verse

Romans 8:28: "We can be so sure that every detail in our lives of love for God is worked into something good."

GOD BRINGS SOMETHING GOOD OUT OF EVERYTHING

God is so good. He loves to work everything out so that it benefits your life and your heart even the hardest things. "The moment we get tired in the waiting, God's Spirit is right alongside helping us along. . . . He knows us far better than we know ourselves . . . and keeps us present before God. That's why we can be so sure that every detail in our lives of love for God is worked into something good" (Romans 8:26-28).

Even when something looks bad or when someone is mean to you, God helps you to look at the evil in other people as an opportunity to show more love. God helps you make this evil bow down to His love in your life. He starts a plan to work good out of this. You always get a happy ending to the wrong that has been done to you, either on earth or when you get to heaven.

For Maria, her calling to act gave Harper the opportunity to act too, because they pursued Maria's word with more purpose. Harper was able to be in a commercial too. Their actions also brought Brooke into a personal relationship with Jesus.

"So, what do you think? With God on our side like this, how can we lose?" (Romans 8:31)

Teacher Notes

_____

_____

_____

_____

_____

_____

_____

_____

_____

_____

_____

_____

_____

_____

_____

_____

Student Question/Reflection

Can you see where God has brought something good out of some of the sad things that have happened in your life?

QUESTION/REFLECTION

Question/Reflection

Can you see where God has brought something good out of some of the sad things that have happened in your life?

WORKBOOK CHAPTER 8 155

_____

_____

_____

_____

_____

_____

_____

 TIP FOR PARENTS:

Engaging your children when they go through something hard is a good mission for every parent. Asking God together to make something good out of a hard situation (they get cut from a team, their best friend moves, they break their arm and can't draw) is important. Showing them that God will work all things for His good and then looking for that good together is an essential training! As a child, I remember when my whole science project collapsed on the way to school, and I was devastated. My mom prayed with me that God would make a way for goodness. When I got home she asked, "Did anything good happen?" I told her that I had asked the teacher if I could do a make-up assignment because mine broke. She understood. I had an extra week. Then I got a brilliant idea about aqueducts from our history class. I made a whole model of the California aqueduct that was really good, if I do say so myself. The other project looked like everyone else's, but my new project was awesome! I got an A+, and to a fourth grader, that was a lesson learned well. I remembered that God was going to turn it for my good. When He did, I recognized it, which reinforced a positive belief pattern of His goodness in my life.

ACTIVATION

INDIVIDUAL ACTIVITY
AND INSTRUCTION

Pick two people in your life who seem to be hard to talk to or who are going through a hard time. Now imagine what they could be like if they were connected to God's heart of love. Pray for that to happen. Write a letter to them that you may never deliver, but it still is a way of praying for them. In the letter, tell them about all the good qualities and gifts you see in them, and what you think God would say or is saying to them. Draw or write out what you think they are called to be and point out the value God has for them.

_____

_____

_____

_____

_____

_____

_____

_____

_____

_____

_____

_____

_____

ACTIVATION, CONTINUED...

GROUP ACTIVITY AND INSTRUCTION

Share stories of when you were given something, but it wasn't just for you—it benefited your family, friends, or even school. What is something you believe God is going to give you that will affect more than just you? Now think about Joseph (in the Bible) and ask God how each person in the group is going to have a life that helps the world.

_____

_____

_____

_____

_____

_____

_____

_____

_____

_____

_____

_____

GROWTH PRAYER

God, I pray that my friendship with You will help people who don't even know You connect to You. Help me share what You are doing in my heart to others. Help me to trust that You will bring good things out of everything in my life, even when it is hard. Show me how to see things through Your eyes so I can see what you are doing and stay encouraged and hopeful.

Amen!

It's time to grow!

ACTIVATION PAGE
I AM CALLED TO HAVE FAVOR AND TO INFLUENCE THOSE AROUND ME, LIKE JOSEPH!

Joseph's father gave him an extravagant coat that had many colors. In the Spirit you wear many virtues—parts of God's character—just like Joseph wore that coat. Color the virtues that are the ones you feel you will operate in and influence people with.

Scripture: He knows us far better than we know ourselves . . . and keeps us present before God. That's why we can be so sure that every detail in our lives of love for God is worked into something good. — Romans 8:26–28

PRINTABLE ACTIVATION PAGE AVAILABLE IN TEACHER REPRODUCIBLE PAGES - PAGE 241

PRINTABLE COLORING PAGE AVAILABLE IN TEACHER REPRODUCIBLE PAGES - PAGE 241

CHAPTER 9 CHECKLIST

☐ Read Chapter 9 in *Growing Up with God*
☐ Choose DVD – Option One or Two
☐ Read aloud: Student testimonials
☐ Review with Students: Synopsis

TEACHING POINT 25:
GOD SPEAKS OUT OF RELATIONSHIP AND GROWS YOUR FRIENDSHIP WITH HIM

☐ Teach / Review Biblical Foundations
Biblical Foundations 9.1:
"Relationship Bring Revelation"

☐ Share: Student Key Verse
Luke 12:4

☐ Teach / Review: Teaching Content 25
God speaks out of relationship and grows your friendship with Him

☐ Student Question / Reflection
If you were going to give yourself a score out of ten, how much would you say you know Jesus right now? What could you do to know Him more?

TEACHING POINT 26:
WHEN GOD ISN'T SPEAKING, IT IS BECAUSE HE WANTS YOU TO GROW IN YOUR IDENTITY

☐ Teach / Review Biblical Foundations
Biblical Foundations 9.2:
"God Loves to Give Us Choice"

☐ Share: Student Key Verse
Galatians 5:16

☐ Teach / Review: Teaching Content 26
When God isn't speaking, it is because He wants you to grow in your identity

☐ Student Question / Reflection
Jesus wants you to know yourself—what you like, how you like it, what your character strengths are, what your personality is like, and how you do things. Why do you think He cares so much about helping you be you?

TEACHING POINT 27:
WHEN YOU ACT LIKE JESUS WITH YOUR FRIENDS, THERE IS ALWAYS A BENEFIT

☐ Teach / Review Biblical Foundations
Biblical Foundations 9.3:
"Becoming Like Jesus"

☐ Share: Student Key Verse
Hebrews 10:24

☐ Teach / Review: Teaching Content 27
When you act like Jesus with your friends, there is always a benefit

☐ Student Question / Reflection
Some kids find that the more they know God, the easier it is to make choices that benefit not just themselves, but the people around them too. Would you agree? Why/why not…

PRAY GROWTH PRAYER

GROWTH ACTIVITIES

☐ Individual
☐ Group
☐ Activity Page
☐ Coloring Page
☐ Implement parenting tip into weekly life

Growing Up with God

CHAPTER

9

TEACHER GUIDE - CHAPTER 9 OVERVIEW

CHAPTER 9 OVERVIEW

☐ Teaching Overview   ☐ DVD Session 9

☐ Chapter Synopsis   ☐ Growth Prayer

TEACHING POINT 25:
GOD SPEAKS OUT OF RELATIONSHIP AND GROWS YOUR FRIENDSHIP WITH HIM

1. Biblical Foundations 9.1:
"Relationship Brings Revelation"

2. Student Key Verse: Luke 12:4

3. Teaching Content 25

4. Student Question: *If you were going to give yourself a score out of ten, how much would you say you know Jesus right now? What could you do to know Him more?*

TEACHING POINT 27:
WHEN YOU ACT LIKE JESUS WITH YOUR FRIENDS, THERE IS ALWAYS A BENEFIT

1. Biblical Foundations 9.3:
"Becoming Like Jesus"

2. Student Key Verse: Hebrews 10:24

3. Teaching Content 27

4. Student Question: *Some kids find that the more they know God, the easier it is to make choices that benefit not just themselves, but the people around them too. Would you agree? Why/why not?*

TEACHING POINT 26:
WHEN GOD ISN'T SPEAKING, IT IS BECUASE HE WANTS YOU TO GROW IN YOUR IDENTITY

1. Biblical Foundations 9.2:
"God Loves to Give Us Choice"

2. Student Key Verse: Galations 5:16

3. Teaching Content 26

4. Student Question: *Jesus wants you to know yourself--what you like, how you like it, what your character strengths are, what your personality is like, and how you do things. Why do you think He cares so much about helping you be you?*

GROWTH ACTIVITIES

1. Individual
2. Group
3. Activity Page
4. Coloring Page
5. Growth Prayer

STORY SYNOPSIS

Brooke has now become a Christian, and she and her family are going to the same church as her new friends. Brooke has a wonderful casting opportunity based on the musical they were in, but she doesn't know what to wear. At Sunday school, the pastor told them God wants to talk to them about everything, so she wants God to tell her what to wear and how to look for the casting director. She isn't hearing anything and is discouraged. Harper and Maria explain to her that God doesn't want to direct her on everything she does. He loves watching her choose because when she's happy being herself, she makes God look amazing. Brooke realizes that she never has to perform for God.

Maria and Harper go with Brooke to her audition so she can feel supported by their friendship. The casting director likes all three of them and lets them all audition. They all get a real acting part in a commercial. Maria's word is coming true. and they end up worshiping together because they're so happy.

CHILD'S TESTIMONY

Basha's Testimony, Age 8

God spoke to me in a dream to not be afraid. In the dream there were dinosaurs chasing me and my family. We got chased into sinking sand (quicksand), and that's when Jesus showed up and turned the sand into water so we could swim out. God showed me that no matter what happens, He will always be there to protect me.

LET'S GET STARTED

Let's jump right into Chapter 9! If you have elected to have your students read each chapter as they go along with the DVDs, then now is the time to read Chapter 9 in *Growing Up with God*. If your students are reading their book outside of your class setting, then please skip down to the teaching points.

PLAY DVD SESSION 9

OPTION 1:

Watch entire Session nine and go back and review all three Teaching Points together.

OPTION 2:

1. Watch the Chapter nine synopsis, Shawn's engaging story, and Teaching Point twenty-five.
2. Pause the DVD for Student Question/Reflection activity.
3. Resume DVD for tTeaching Point twenty-six.
4. Pause the DVD for Student Question/Reflection activity.
5. Resume DVD for Teaching Point twenty-seven.
6. Pause the DVD for Student Question/Reflection activity.

GROWTH PRAYER
PRAY ALONG WITH SHAWN ON THE DVD GROWTH PRAYER

God, I pray that You would help me discover my identity more and more. Help me to walk in the character of this great identity. Thank you for trusting me to make some important decisions, and I pray that I would feel Your heart of joy when I make them. Also, help my relationships benefit from my relationship with You.

Amen!

Let's grow up in God!

Teacher Notes:

_____

_____

_____

_____

_____

_____

_____

_____

Teaching Point 25

GOD SPEAKS OUT OF RELATIONSHIP AND GROWS YOUR FRIENDSHIP WITH HIM

GOD SPEAKS OUT OF RELATIONSHIP AND GROWS YOUR FRIENDSHIP WITH HIM

TEACHING POINT 25

1. Biblical Foundations 9.1:
"Relationship Brings Revelation"
2. Student Key Verse: Luke 12:4
3. Teaching Content 25
4. Student Question: *If you were going to give yourself a score out of ten, how much would you say you know Jesus right now? What could you do to know Him more?*

9.1 BIBLICAL FOUNDATIONS: RELATIONSHIPS BRING REVELATION

John, Jesus's favorite disciple, cared for God's heart. The Bible says that while they were hanging out, John was so close to Jesus that he laid his head on His chest in just intimacy and cuddled. How close was John to Jesus? Pretty close, I would say! Only close friends get to rest their head on the chest/heart of God and ask questions. When you are close to someone, you don't need to yell for them to hear. You can whisper and they can hear. God wants to whisper things to you. As you lean in really closely to His heart, you will grow in relationship with Him.

"One of His disciples, whom Jesus loved (esteemed), was leaning against Jesus' chest."
— John 13:23 AMP

Student Key Verse
Luke 12:4: "I'm speaking to you as dear friends."

GOD SPEAKS OUT OF RELATIONSHIP AND GROWS YOUR FRIENDSHIP WITH HIM

God loves talking to you, but you won't understand Him if you don't get to know him. God loves to talk to you and tell you what is in His heart. Hearing a prophetic word or just knowing the Bible is not enough. You have to know Him! You have to have a friendship connection with Him. Have you ever had friends that you knew so well, you knew what they were thinking the moment that you watched a funny scene in a movie together? You have inside jokes and a friendship connection that has been built out of your history together. God wants to make history with you!

"I'm speaking to you as dear friends" (Luke 12:4). "People who don't know God and the way he works fuss over these things, but you know both God and how he works. Steep yourself in God-reality, God-initiative, God-provisions. You'll find all your everyday human concerns will be met. Don't be afraid of missing out. You're my dearest friends! The Father wants to give you the very kingdom itself" (Luke 12:29-32). Spend time with God. Talk to Him, listen to Him, and be ready to notice things He points out to you in your day. Write down your prayers and what He says about them in a journal. Spend time outside and ask Him about His creation. See if any numbers or words stand out, and ask Him why.

Every moment you spend connecting with God helps that connection to grow. Every time you practice hearing Him and seeing what He shows you, you learn how to see and hear more clearly. It's what God has always wanted—to be your best friend and share everything about Himself with you.

Teacher Notes

_____
_____
_____
_____
_____
_____
_____
_____
_____
_____
_____
_____
_____
_____
_____
_____
_____
_____
_____

Student
Question/Reflection

If you were going to give yourself a score out of ten, how much would you say you know Jesus right now? What could you do to know him more?

_____

_____

_____

_____

_____

_____

_____

_____

QUESTION/REFLECTION

Question/Reflection

If you were going to give yourself a score out of ten, how much would you say you know Jesus right now? What could you do to know him more?

_____

_____

_____

_____

_____

_____

_____

WORKBOOK CHAPTER 9 **167**

_____

_____

_____

_____

_____

_____

_____

_____

_____

_____

_____

Teaching Point 26

WHEN GOD ISN'T SPEAKING, IT IS BECAUSE HE WANTS YOU TO GROW IN YOUR IDENTITY

WHEN GOD ISN'T SPEAKING, IT IS BECAUSE HE WANTS YOU TO GROW IN YOUR IDENTITY

TEACHING POINT 26

1. Biblical Foundations 9.2:
"God Loves to Give Us Choice"
2. Student Key Verse: Galations 5:16
3. Teaching Content 26
4. Student Question: *Jesus wants you to know yourself--what you like, how you like it, what your character strengths are, what your personality is like, and how you do things. Why do you think He cares so much about helping you be you?*

9.2 BIBLICAL FOUNDATIONS: GOD LOVES TO GIVE US CHOICE

When God created you and me, He put inside us a "will" and a desire to choose. He did not create robots! He wants our daily involvement. He takes great pleasure when we are faced with many options and we decide to choose Him. God speaks directly to us a lot, but sometimes He doesn't need to. Why? Because we need to mature in our faith and actually walk out all of the things God has planned for us. Be encouraged when He is speaking and when He is silent! You are maturing in your faith every day!

"Readily recognize what he wants from you, and quickly respond to it. Unlike the culture around you, always dragging you down to its level of immaturity, God brings the best out of you, develops well-formed maturity in you" (Romans 12:2).

Student Key Verse

Galatians 5:16: "Live freely, animated and motivated by God's Spirit."

WHEN GOD ISN'T SPEAKING, IT IS BECAUSE HE WANTS YOU TO GROW IN YOUR IDENTITY

God speaks sometimes to share His heart with you, instruct you, amuse you, help you, connect to you, or encourage you. Over time, your friendship with Him matures and you start to understand exactly who He made you to be. This is called building your personal identity with God. Your identity is the sum of who you are. When you know yourself, you know what you are good at, what you enjoy, how you see things, how you communicate with others, and what your personality type is. You know how to pursue the great things in life, not just settle for good things. You do life out of your whole self, not just the parts you think people want to see.

You also choose to do wonderful things out of your own free will. This was God's design all along—to have mature sons and daughters who do things and go places because it's a natural part of who they are. He's never wanted to boss you around. The more you mature you become, the less you need instruction or direction. You just know what to do. Some people are waiting for God to talk to them and tell them what to do about everything—even what to eat for lunch! This usually happens because they don't know who they are, and they don't know God all that well yet either.

God trusted Paul to choose where he wanted to be: "As long as I'm alive in this body, there is good work for me to do. If I had to choose right now, I hardly know which I'd choose. Hard choice! . . . I plan to be around awhile, companion to you as your growth and joy in this life of trusting God continues." (Philippians 1:22-25) Paul said to "Live freely, animated and motivated by God's Spirit" (Galatians 5:16). You have the freedom to make all the choices you want. It brings God glory when you make great choices. It makes His character in you look so beautiful. He doesn't always tell you what to do because He wants to show the world that you are powerful and you have chosen a life in Him that is strong and empowered!

Teacher Notes

Student Question/Reflection

Jesus wants you to know yourself—what you like, how you like it, what your character strengths are, what your personality is like, how you do things. Why do you think he cares so much about helping you be you?

QUESTION/REFLECTION

Question/Reflection

Jesus wants you to know yourself—what you like, how you like it, what your character strengths are, what your personality is like, how you do things. Why do you think he cares so much about helping you be you?

WORKBOOK CHAPTER 9 171

TIP FOR PARENTS:

This is a perfect time to talk to your children about things they are making decisions about that honor you. Talk about what you love that they do. Think of 2-5 things that they chose today (clothes they wore, activities to be involved in, helped by doing dishes without you asking, or something bigger), and encourage them about how they are maturing and growing. Now ask them if there is anything that they feel they are growing in spiritually/in God—something that is shows their maturity. Like—do they read their Bible more, or pray without having to be told, or reach out to people without waiting to hear from God? These are the types of ways they can begin to track their maturity, and when you point out areas that they are maturing in, it will build their self-confidence.

Teaching Point 27

WHEN YOU ACT LIKE JESUS WITH YOUR FRIENDS, THERE IS ALWAYS A BENEFIT

WHEN YOU ACT LIKE JESUS WITH YOUR FRIENDS, THERE IS ALWAYS A BENEFIT

TEACHING POINT 27

1. Biblical Foundations 9.3:
"Becoming Like Jesus"
2. Student Key Verse: Hebrews 10:24
3. Teaching Content 27
4. Student Question: *Some kids find that the more they know God, the easier it is to make choices that benefit not just themselves, but the people around them too. Would you agree? Why/why not?*

9.3 BIBLICAL FOUNDATIONS: BECOMING LIKE JESUS

When we accept Jesus in our heart and believe in Him, we can now live like Him. Every time you are gracious, loving, and forgiving, the benefits of the kingdom of heaven are released. We actually partner with God every time we decide to love. It is like we are holding hands with Jesus and doing what He would do in the world around us. If we act like Jesus and do the wonderful things that He did, then our friends will benefit from God's love.

"Think of yourselves the way Christ Jesus thought of himself." — Philippians 2:5

Student Key Verse

Hebrews 10:24: "Let's see how inventive we can be in encouraging love and helping out . . . spurring each other on."

WHEN YOU ACT LIKE JESUS WITH YOUR FRIENDS, THERE IS ALWAYS A BENEFIT

The beautiful thing about real relationships is that you help each other become better people. Your times of connecting aren't just for fun and companionship. You become more of your true, God-given self as you spend time with the right people. A young girl we know began to help autistic kids who were in a program that ran alongside their art class at school. She got kids to volunteer and she paired each one with an autistic kid for the art class. Through this amazing program, all of her friends learned how amazing these children who had autism were. She helped give dignity and understanding to kids who were sometimes ignored or forgotten. In her school today, most of the kids now have autistic friends, and there is very little stigma on being autistic. Your promises from God even affect your family and friends, and they add to what God is showing you.

"So let's do it—full of belief, confident that we're presentable inside and out. Let's keep a firm grip on the promises that keep us going. He always keeps his word. Let's see how inventive we can be in encouraging love and helping out . . . spurring each other on" (Hebrews 10:24). You actually are supposed to be creative and inventive in your life and relationships! Remember that Brooke's friendship with Maria and Harper meant they unexpectedly got to act in a commercial with her. You being you in your strength, personality, and relationship with God actually helps your friends have open doors to opportunities too. Greatness happens when Jesus is in the center of your friendships!

As you grow up in God, you start to see how being a part of His family actually gives you other opportunities that you would have never had. You all can't help but help each other achieve great things and be great people!

Teacher Notes

Student Question/Reflection

Some kids find that the more they know God, the easier it is to make choices that benefit not just themselves, but the people around them too. Would you agree? Why/why not?

Hebrews 10:24 says you can be confident inside and out. Among your classmates or in your family, what people do you think are like that, and what do you think helps them to be comfortable being themselves?

_____

_____

_____

_____

QUESTION/REFLECTION

Question/Reflection

Some kids find that the more they know God, the easier it is to make choices that benefit not just themselves, but the people around them too. Would you agree? Why/why not...

WORKBOOK CHAPTER 9 **175**

ACTIVATION

INDIVIDUAL ACTIVITY
AND INSTRUCTION

Make a list of the fruits of the Holy Spirit you'd like to grow in, and write at least three of these words down. For example: patience, peace, love, happiness, self-control, humility, sharing, and selflessness. Then ask God to show you each time you might have an opportunity to grow during the week and write it down next to the word. We grow when we see our need to grow!

_____

_____

_____

_____

_____

_____

_____

_____

_____

_____

_____

_____

_____

ACTIVATION, CONTINUED...

GROUP ACTIVITY AND INSTRUCTION

Discuss what choices people in the group are good at making—decisions they don't need help with but someone else facing the same situation might. What are things that they can do right now without adult help because they have skill and training? Celebrate one accomplishment of each person in the group . . . and show photos, medals, short videos, etc. if you have them. Then encourage each other about those accomplishments, even if they happened several years ago.

_____

_____

_____

_____

_____

_____

_____

_____

_____

_____

_____

_____

GROWTH PRAYER

God, I pray that You would help me discover my identity more and more. Help me to walk in the character of this great identity. Thank You for trusting me to make some important decisions, and I pray that I would feel Your heart of joy when I make them. Also, help my relationships benefit from my relationship with You.

Amen!

Let's grow up in God!

ACTIVATION PAGE
THE HOLY SPIRIT IS NOT A JUNIOR IN ME, BUT A FULL HOLY SPIRIT!

God is not limited to our size or maturity. Write words that describe what you can grow in—God will help you practice listening to the Holy Spirit and growing in love. For example: "I can prophesy." "I can heal the sick." "I can listen." "I can pray for people." "I can intercede." "I can create." "I can love." "I can share my faith."

Scripture: So let's do it—full of belief, confident that we're presentable inside and out. Let's keep a firm grip on the promises that keep us going. He always keeps his word. Let's see how inventive we can be in encouraging love and helping out . . . spurring each other on.
— Hebrews 10:22-24

PRINTABLE ACTIVATION PAGE AVAILABLE IN TEACHER REPRODUCIBLE PAGES - PAGE 241

PRINTABLE COLORING PAGE AVAILABLE IN TEACHER REPRODUCIBLE PAGES · PAGE 241

CHAPTER 10 CHECKLIST

- ☐ Read Chapter 10 in *Growing Up with God*
- ☐ Choose DVD – Option One or Two
- ☐ Read aloud: Student testimonials
- ☐ Review with Students: Synopsis

TEACHING POINT 28:
YOU CAN LOVE WELL

- ☐ Teach / Review Biblical Foundations
  Biblical Foundations 10.1:
  "Loving Well Is a Choice"
- ☐ Share: Student Key Verse
  John 3:16-17
- ☐ Teach / Review: Teaching Content 28
  You can love well
- ☐ Student Question / Reflection
  When you think of people who show you God's love, how do they show it? Is it through preaching or through treating you in a certain way?

TEACHING POINT 29:
THE NUMBER-ONE WAY PEOPLE BECOME CHRISTIANS IS THROUGH RELATIONSHIP

- ☐ Teach / Review Biblical Foundations
  Biblical Foundations 10.2:
  "Healthy Relationship Is Important"
- ☐ Share: Student Key Verse
  1 John 4:19
- ☐ Teach / Review: Teaching Content 29
  The number one way people become christians is through relationship
- ☐ Student Question / Reflection
  What do you think is the main thing your family and friends need from you? How much of it do you need Jesus's help with?

TEACHING POINT 30:
YOU GROW IN GOD EVERY DAY

- ☐ Teach / Review Biblical Foundations
  Biblical Foundations 10.3:
  "Daily Walk with God"
- ☐ Share: Student Key Verse
  Galatians 5:22-23
- ☐ Teach / Review: Teaching Content 30
  You grow in God every day
- ☐ Student Question / Reflection
  How long do you think it takes to grow up in God so much that you end up being just like Jesus? God grows some things quickly and other things slowly. How do you know if you are growing up in God already? Do you know He loves you just as much now as He will when you have grown up in Him? That's how amazing His love is.

PRAY GROWTH PRAYER

GROWTH ACTIVITIES

- ☐ Individual
- ☐ Group
- ☐ Activity Page
- ☐ Coloring Page
- ☐ Implement parenting tip into weekly life

Growing Up with God

CHAPTER

10

TEACHER GUIDE - CHAPTER 10 OVERVIEW

CHAPTER 10 OVERVIEW

- ☐ Teaching Overview
- ☐ Chapter Synopsis
- ☐ DVD Session 10
- ☐ Growth Prayer

TEACHING POINT 28:
YOU CAN LOVE WELL

1. Biblical Foundations 10.1:
"Loving Well Is a Choice"

2. Student Key Verse: John 3:16-17

3. Teaching Content 28

4. Student Question: *When you think of people who show you God's love, how do they show it? Is it through preaching or through treating you in a certain way?*

TEACHING POINT 30:
YOU GROW IN GOD EVERY DAY

1. Biblical Foundations 10.3:
"Daily Walk with God

2. Student Key Verse: Galations 5:22-23

3. Teaching Content 30

4. Student Question: *How long do you think it takes to grow up in God so much that you end up being just like Jesus? God grows some things quickly and other things slowly. How do you know if you are growing up in God already? Do you know He loves you just as much now as He will when you have grown up in Him? That's how amazing His love is.*

TEACHING POINT 29:
THE NUMBER-ONE WAY PEOPLE BECOME CHRISTIANS IS THROUGH RELATIONSHIP

1. Biblical Foundations 10.2:
"Healthy Relationship is Important"

2. Student Key Verse: 1 John 4:19

3. Teaching Content 29

4. Student Question: *What do you think is the main thing your family and friends need from you? How much of it do you need Jesus' help with?*

GROWTH ACTIVITIES

1. Individual
2. Group
3. Activity Page
4. Coloring Page
5. Growth Prayer

STORY SYNOPSIS

The kids are in kid's church, listening to the pastor share his message. He is sharing about how the Holy Spirit reveals the deepest parts of the heart of God to our hearts and ties them together. He does this so that we can hear from God and feel what He feels and know what He knows. He shares how his parents, who have been married a long time, use fewer words while they're working together in the kitchen. He says that's because they know each other and love each other so well.

Harper and Maria feel that way about their friendship. Then Jamal tells Lucas that he has made him feel this way too. It's made Jamal think maybe there really is a God, and he wants to grow up in God too! The four friends pray for him with the pastor, and Jamal invites Jesus to be his friend.

At Maria's house that summer, they notice Hartley practicing how to listen to God as well. They discover that you don't have to wait for a meeting or church to grow up with God. It happens every day for any age

CHILD'S TESTIMONY

Hailey's Testimony, Age 10

When I first started hearing from God, me and my parents were learning together. Kind of a funny story: I have a fish in a small tank on my desk. It died and my mom and dad replaced it with one that looks just like it but did not tell me. One night I had a dream that my fish had died and been replaced without me knowing. I got up and told my mom my dream, and she looked at me weird and asked, "God gave you that dream?" Then she said, "Hailey, we did replace your fish with one that looks just like your old one, but we did not tell you because we did not want you to be sad." I felt sad about my fish, but my parents explained that God was teaching them that God speaks to kids just like He speaks to adults. I think God is teaching my parents more about my gift than me.

LET'S GET STARTED

Let's jump right into Chapter 10! If you have elected to have your students read each chapter as they go along with the DVDs, then now is the time to read Chapter 10 in *Growing Up with God*. If your students are reading their book outside of your class setting, then please skip down to the teaching points.

PLAY DVD SESSION 10

OPTION 1:

Watch entire Session ten and go back and review all three Teaching Points together.

OPTION 2:

1. Watch the Chapter ten synopsis, Shawn's engaging story, and Teaching Point twenty-eight.
2. Pause the DVD for Student Question/Reflection activity.
3. Resume DVD for Teaching Point twenty-nine.
4. Pause the DVD for Student Question/Reflection activity.
5. Resume DVD for Teaching Point thirty.
6. Pause the DVD for Student Question/Reflection activity.

GROWTH PRAYER
PRAY ALONG WITH SHAWN ON THE DVD GROWTH PRAYER

God, teach me how to love well. I pray that as I love people, they will get to know You. I pray that some will become Christians because of Your love for me and my love for You! Please help me to grow daily with You.

Amen!

It's time to grow in God! You are doing it, and you are going to be a giant in His love!

Teacher Notes:

_____

_____

_____

_____

_____

_____

_____

_____

Teaching Point 28
YOU CAN LOVE WELL

YOU CAN LOVE WELL

TEACHING POINT 28

1. Biblical Foundations 10.1:
"Loving Well Is a Choice"
2. Student Key Verse: John 3:16-17
3. Teaching Content 28
4. Student Question: *When you think of people who show you God's love, how do they show it? Is it through preaching or through treating you in a certain way?*

10.1 BIBLICAL FOUNDATIONS: LOVING WELL IS A CHOICE

We may not always agree with what others say, but we need to love them anyway. If we are intentional every day about putting others before ourselves, then we will master love like Jesus. Jesus laid down His life for us. We should consider laying down our pride, our opinions, and our perceptions to make way for others to be loved. You are powerful when you love! "Welcome with open arms fellow believers who don't see things the way you do. And don't jump all over them every time they do or say something you don't agree with—even when it seems that they are strong on opinions but weak in the faith department. Remember, they have their own history to deal with. Treat them gently" (Romans 14:1).

Student Key Verse

John 3:16-17: "God [went] to all the trouble of sending his Son ... to help, to put the world right again."

YOU CAN LOVE WELL

You are called to love people just like God sent Jesus to love them. This love has an invitation in it, not a command. You can't force anyone to believe what you believe, but you do get to love them. Regardless of their beliefs, they are worthy of love!

Jesus treated all the people around Him as if they were worthy of going to heaven, whether they believed in Him or not. He loved them as though they had full value! This is how you are supposed to love! You can try and share your faith, but you aren't responsible to actually get people saved. Only God can do that. What you do get to be, though, is an example of His love.

"This is how much God loved the world: He gave his Son, his one and only Son. And this is why: so that no one need be destroyed; by believing in him, anyone can have a whole and lasting life. God didn't go to all the trouble of sending his Son merely to point an accusing finger, telling the world how bad it was. He came to help, to put the world right again" (John 3:16-17). You don't get to condemn anyone for not believing, but you can treat him or her like family.

Sometimes you love God so much that you want everyone around you to know how good He is, but instead of building relationships and friendships with people, you just preach to them. That doesn't help anyone most of the time, because people will connect to God's love through you before you even use words. Once they feel as if they can trust you and you feel like a friend to them, then you get to share. The more you are growing up with God, the more you grow in love for others. People can feel that love in real ways, and they will connect to you more because of it, even if they don't agree with your beliefs.

Teacher Notes

_____
_____
_____
_____
_____
_____
_____
_____
_____
_____
_____
_____
_____
_____
_____
_____
_____
_____

Student
Question/Reflection

When you think of people who show you God's love, how do they show it? Is it through preaching or through treating you in a certain way?

_____

_____

_____

_____

_____

_____

_____

QUESTION/REFLECTION

Question/Reflection

When you think of people who show you God's love, how do they show it? Is it through preaching or through treating you in a certain way?

_____

_____

_____

_____

_____

_____

_____

_____

_____

_____

_____

_____

WORKBOOK CHAPTER 10 **187**

Teaching Point 29

THE NUMBER-ONE WAY PEOPLE BECOME CHRISTIANS IS THROUGH RELATIONSHIP

THE NUMBER-ONE WAY PEOPLE
BECOME CHRISTIANS IS THROUGH RELATIONSHIP

TEACHING POINT 29

1. Biblical Foundations 10.2:
"Healthy Relationship is Important"
2. Student Key Verse: 1 John 4:19
3. Teaching Content 29
4. Student Question: *What do you think is the main thing your family and friends need from you? How much of it do you need Jesus' help with?*

10.2 BIBLICAL FOUNDATIONS:
HEALTHY RELATIONSHIP IS IMPORTANT

Jesus was in such a good relationship with Father God that He was able to bring salvation to the world! Jesus and His Father talked every day, sharing the desires of their hearts and making plans to bring them about. It was out of this healthy relationship that so many were brought into their fullness. Jesus was as impactful as He was because of His relationship with Father God. Imagine what your healthy relationships can do in the world around you! You can be Jesus to the world around you and lead your friends to God. Remember, people only care what you know when they know that you care. "Jesus said, 'I am the Road, also the Truth, also the Life. No one gets to the Father apart from me. If you really knew me, you would know my Father as well. From now on, you do know him. You've even seen him!'" (John 14:6–7)

Student Key Verse

1 John 4:19: "First we were loved, now we love."

THE NUMBER-ONE WAY PEOPLE BECOME CHRISTIANS IS THROUGH RELATIONSHIP

People will come to Jesus through your relationship with them. Sometimes churches go out and do wonderful evangelism outreaches, or cook a meal and give it to the homeless, or travel to other countries on school evangelism trips. These are important, but the primary way you are called to share your faith is to do it every day through your love.

"God is love. When we take up permanent residence in a life of love, we live in God and God lives in us. This way, love has the run of the house, becomes at home and mature in us, so that we're free of worry on Judgment Day—your standing in the world is identical with Christ's. There is no room in love for fear. Well-formed love banishes fear. Since fear is crippling, a fearful life—fear of death, fear of judgment—is one not yet fully formed in love. We, though, are going to love—love and be loved. First we were loved, now we love. He loved us first" (1 John 4: 17-19).

Jesus said that to really grow up in God, you need to do two things: "The first in importance is, 'Listen, Israel: The Lord your God is one; so love the Lord God with all your passion and prayer and intelligence and energy.' And here is the second: 'Love others as well as you love yourself'" (Mark 12:29-30). Think about that. You like to make sure you get enough to eat, rides to your friends' houses, and help from your friends and family when you need it. When you love others as well as you love yourself, you spend as much time making sure their needs are met as you do your own.

When you live in love for God, people can feel that you are living differently. You get to invite people to see God by the way you love. When they experience love through you every single day for months, and even years, it makes them know for sure that God's love is real!

Teacher Notes

Student Question/Reflection

When you think of people who show you God's love, how do they show it? Is it through preaching or through treating you like family?

What do you think is the main thing your family and friends need from you? How much of it do you need Jesus's help with?

💡 TIP FOR PARENTS:

Almost all kids are going to have relationships or become friends with people who don't believe, or even get to know Christians who have different foundational/doctrinal beliefs. It is so important that we reinforce that everyone is worthy of love and that boundaries are a way of supporting healthy love. Sometimes parents focus so much on boundaries that it creates an "us and them" mentality. Kids become confused about whether they should be protecting their hearts or loving people. Our goal isn't to create rules on who not to connect to; our goal is to teach kids how to connect and when to not connect (when it will compromise their character or peace). Children will learn as much from their nonreligious friends as from their religious friends. Creating truly powerful people only happens when children learn how to protect their love and heart in the midst of all kinds of good and bad choices. Are you involved in your children's relationships? Their world is most likely small, so there are probably 2-5 people who deeply influence them outside of your house. Try and plan some friendship time with your kids and their friends. Engage them in fun ways and talk to them about their families and lives. When you are a part of your children's friendship circle because you are showing real interest, your children will be more likely to share their heart with you about those friends.

Teaching Point 30
YOU GROW IN GOD EVERY DAY

YOU GROW IN GOD EVERY DAY

TEACHING POINT 30

1. Biblical Foundations 10.3:
"Daily Walk with God

2. Student Key Verse: Galations 5:22-23

3. Teaching Content 30

4. Student Question: *How long do you think it takes to grow up in God so much that you end up being just like Jesus? God grows some things quickly and other things slowly. How do you know if you are growing up in God already? Do you know He loves you just as much now as He will when you have grown up in Him? That's how amazing His love is.*

10.3 BIBLICAL FOUNDATIONS: DAILY WALK WITH GOD

We have been invited on an amazing journey of growing up with God on a daily basis. We are set apart by God as chosen and loved. This daily connection with God is our partnership with his Heart. God has placed all the resources of heaven at our fingertips so we can grow in grace and knowledge in how to live the best life possible--through our relationship with Him. In the big and the small, we can discover Him in all things and be transformed into His image. We are constantly being perfected in His image as he renews us day by day! Grow up with God daily, and have fun doing it! "But grow in the grace and knowledge of our Lord and Savior Jesus Christ. To Him be the glory, both now and to the day of eternity. Amen" (2 Peter 3:18 NASB).

Student Key Verse

Galatians 5:22-23: "The fruit of the Spirit is love, joy, peace, patience, kindness, goodness, faithfulness, gentleness, self-control" (NASB).

YOU GROW IN GOD EVERY DAY

You don't have to grow just in a few spurts at meetings, church, or camps. You get to grow every day through how you make choices. You will know you are growing in God by the changes that happen in your heart! Just like fruit trees grow fruit every year, your life will start to have character and you'll feel comfortable and happy being you. You will have the ability to really know what God is saying to you, and people around you will benefit from all that spiritual fruit. You will be able to measure how different you are because you will have characteristics of God's love.

Paul explained how to check if you are growing: "But what happens when we live God's way? He brings gifts into our lives, much the same way that fruit appears in an orchard—things like affection for others, exuberance about life, serenity. We develop a willingness to stick with things, a sense of compassion in the heart, and a conviction that a basic holiness permeates things and people. We find ourselves involved in loyal commitments, not needing to force our way in life, able to marshal and direct our energies wisely" (Galatians 5: 22-23).

You will have the fruits of the Spirit, and there's nothing God loves more than giving that fruit away to the hungry. The more they get to taste of His love and kindness through His people, the more they'll want. They'll know that it's the kind of love that doesn't come from people. It's a heavenly love. "I'm spreading a banquet of Tree-of-Life fruit, a supper plucked from God's orchard" (Revelation 2:7). Even if you find it hard to love people now, God's love will fill your heart so much that it will grow ten sizes bigger and then you'll find it easy to be just like Jesus.

Student Question/Reflection

How long do you think it takes to grow up in God, so much so that you end up being just like Jesus? God grows some things quickly and other things slowly. How do you know if you are growing up in God already? Do you know he loves you just as much now as he will when you have grown up in him? That's how amazing his love is.

QUESTION/REFLECTION

Question/Reflection

How long do you think it takes to grow up in God so much that you end up being just like Jesus? God grows some things quickly and other things slowly. How do you know if you are growing up in God already? Do you know he loves you just as much now as he will when you have grown up in him? That's how amazing his love is.

WORKBOOK CHAPTER 10 195

_____

_____

_____

_____

_____

_____

TIP FOR PARENTS:

Your kids need to spend time with God with you. This is a missing art in families in the church today. We rely on our church, our social media, and our programs to model spiritual culture to our children, but they need us. Praying together with our kids is essential for them to learn how to value prayer, and not just bedtime prayers for protection and health. Use that same time every night to share together what you want God to do in your lives and then pray big prayers about real things. We know God's intention is to keep us safe and to keep us healthy, so we don't necessarily need to pray those things when we have a Bible filled with God's intention to do just that. We do, however, need to articulate our heart in real relationship to God. Families that pray together stay together! Use all the times of prayer to be real times of prayer.

My friend's family of six uses dinner-time prayer to each articulate something they are truly thankful for. Each prayer is personal, and then together they ask God to help them have more faith for more goodness! I love this because it's engaging and trackable, not just a time of well-intentioned prayers.

ACTIVATION

INDIVIDUAL ACTIVITY AND INSTRUCTION

LOVE LETTER WEEK: Write down a spiritual note, encouragement, or letter for each person in your family that they can read quickly each day for seven days. Post them on the bathroom mirror or fridge, or even leave some on their pillows. Try and encourage them with a Scripture, and tell them something you love about them.

_____

_____

_____

_____

_____

_____

_____

_____

_____

_____

_____

_____

_____

_____

_____

_____

ACTIVATION, CONTINUED...

GROUP ACTIVITY AND INSTRUCTION

Break up into groups of two. Share your faith with the other person as if he or she doesn't know Jesus. Try and be as real and heartfelt as possible. Then pray with the person to receive Jesus (use the prayer in *Growing Up with God* if you need the tool).

_____

_____

_____

_____

_____

_____

_____

_____

_____

_____

_____

_____

_____

_____

_____

GROWTH PRAYER

God, teach me how to love well. I pray that as I love people, they will get to know You. I pray that some will become Christians because of Your love for me and my love for You! Please help me to grow daily with You.

Amen!

It's time to grow in God! You are doing it, and you are going to be a giant in His love!

ACTIVATION PAGE
I CAN GROW IN CLOSENESS TO GOD!

Draw yourself into the picture, and with it, show how close you feel to Jesus. For example: Are you holding hands, are you standing close, are you far off? Don't worry if you aren't close yet; relationship takes time! If you are close, you can get even closer! In *Growing Up with God*, the friends share how much closer they have gotten since the class started. Write words beside the picture you drew of yourself that describe your closeness to Jesus.

Scripture: We, though, are going to love—love and be loved. First we were loved, now we love. He loved us first. — 1 John 4: 17–19

PRINTABLE ACTIVATION PAGE AVAILABLE IN TEACHER REPRODUCIBLE PAGES · PAGE 241

PRINTABLE COLORING PAGE AVAILABLE IN TEACHER REPRODUCIBLE PAGES - PAGE 241

GLOSSARY

A BLESSING/TO BLESS – To make someone else's life happy, joyous, and full. To bless means to provide for another person's needs no matter what the situation is. Blessings also come from God and are similar to God's "gifts."

ADVICE – Kind words of guidance and comfort that help people when they are struggling with a difficult time. Advice helps people make good decisions.

AFFECTIONATE – To be loving, tender, and caring.

APPRECIATION – Being thankful for someone or something; having a thankful heart for all of the blessings God has provided in your life.

ASSISTANCE – To give help to or get help from another person. It is okay to ask for assistance when you are struggling. There are plenty of people around you who love to give you help.

ATHLETIC – Physically active and strong. Someone who enjoys playing sports and is good at it. Someone who loves to compete and has fun doing it. Soccer players are an example of people who are athletic.

ATMOSPHERE/CULTURE OF LOVE – It's when your surroundings are so influenced by love that love can't help but be cultivated and embraced.

AUDITION – To try out for something.

BELIEF – When you have a lot of faith and confidence in something.

BIBLE – A very special book written by God's Spirit through men on earth. The Bible gives us a glimpse of what it means to love God and one another. The Bible tells people that Jesus is the way to heaven and the key to living a happy and purposed life on earth.

BODY OF CHRIST – You and your family and those who love Jesus are the body of Christ. The body of Christ believes that Jesus is the Son of God and the body of Christ works together to serve God in different ways.

CALLINGS – The plans and desires that God has planted in your heart. They will lead you and encourage you to make the world a better place to live in.

CHEERFUL GIVER – One who has a positive attitude and loves to do things to help others. One who recognizes that all of the good things we have in life are from God and that it pleases Him when we share with others. For example, if you love nutrition, you can create many recipes in order to create healthy meals for people. Chefs can release life through the food they provide.

CHURCH – A place where people come together and sing songs to God, learn about God, and spend time together honoring God.

CIRCUMSTANCE – An event or situation that you might find yourself in. It can be good or bad, but in every circumstance we have to remember to trust God and ask Him to guide us.

CO-LABOR – To work together with someone.

COMMANDMENTS – Rules that were made with love. When we follow God's commandments, He is very happy and our lives will be blessed.

COMMUNICATION – To talk to someone in person, on the phone, or through the mail; to share a message over the TV, online, in a movie, or over the radio.

COMPANIONSHIP – It is a feeling you get when you are close with your friends.

COMPASSIONATE – This is what you feel when you show concern to others and your friends over what they are going through.

COUNSELORS – People who gather wisdom from the heart of God and help guide people to the correct path for their lives. Counselors help people through tough times and in happy times. They are similar to teachers and pastors.

COURAGEOUS – Fearlessness; we can be courageous because we know that God is with us all the time. It means doing the right thing even when it seems too hard.

CREATIVITY – To design and make new and original pieces of beauty by doing things like writing books, making up dances, painting, or sculpting. Creativity is a gift from God and adds joy and life to the world.

CULTURE – The beliefs and customs of a nation or people. Culture creates a standard of thought and feelings for people to live by, i.e., a culture of love and honor.

DESIRE – An emotion that expresses wanting something; it can express the feeling of caring and compassion that God put within us. God also has desires. For example, God desires us to love Him and others.

DISCERNMENT – To have a good sense of the things going on around you and to be aware of your surroundings. Discernment helps you make good decisions. It is important to have this quality so that you act with love and honor, which furthers the kingdom of God.

DISCIPLINE – To consistently obey rules or a set of behaviors for one's benefit.

EARTHLY FATHER – The father that the Lord gave you who watches over you, instructs you, and protects you on earth. God made earthly fathers to be a good example of what God is like.

EMOTIONS – The feelings you get inside such as happiness, sadness, anger, excitement, or loneliness. People such as school counselors help others understand and deal with their emotions. Emotions are usually a response to an event in your life, and it is important to talk with God about your emotions because He loves to know how you feel. Jesus is the best counselor.

ENCOURAGER – Someone who lifts another person up with his words. Encouragers are kind and compassionate and they support their friends in every way they can. They have a positive attitude and are ready to help whenever they are needed.

ENEMIES – People who try to harm you. God tells us to forgive our enemies and show them love, even when it is hard.

EVERLASTING LIFE – Is when we embrace the salvation God offers us today and we live with Jesus for all of eternity.

EVEN-TEMPERED – This is someone is not easily angered but often calm and peaceful.

FAITH – Is complete trust and confidence in something or someone, like when you fully believe in God.

FAITHFUL – To be reliable and trustworthy; to obey what God tells you to do.

FREEDOM – The ability to do whatever you want. True freedom is following God's plan and living under His protective and watchful care. God has given us freedom to make our own choices, and He wants each and every person to use that freedom to spread love throughout the world.

FRIENDS – These are people you are close to and have a bond with, people you get to journey through life with.

FRUIT OF GOOD WORK – When you do good actions and help those in need, amazing things will happen in your life. God rewards those serve Him with "good fruit." All who listen to Him and take care of His children will be blessed greatly by God.

FRUITS OF THE SPIRIT – In Galatians 5:22, God talks about different character traits that we get to walk in as children of God. These traits are love, joy, peace, forbearance, kindness, goodness, faithfulness, gentleness. and self-control.

GENERATIONS – The amount of time between the birth of a parent and the birth of his children, usually between eighteen and twenty-five years.

GENEROUS – This is when you show great kindness to someone by giving your time, finances, or other resources.

GIFTS – God has given every single person on the earth one or more special gifts. It is up to you to pray to God and ask Him what special gift He has given you and then use that gift to make the world a better place. God has also given us many other gifts, like life on earth, our family, and Jesus.

GLORY – To give great praise and honor to someone. For example, King David had a director of music that helped him to sing about the glory of God and creation. Glory is a positive thing as it can show forth the beauty of all that God has done.

GOD – He is the One who created everything, including you! He is a Father.

GOD-ACTS – Things God does that we couldn't do on our own. We also call these miracles, signs, and wonders.

GOD JOURNEY – This is when you go on a fun adventure, a journey with God that He guides you on.

GOD'S CHILDREN – All of humanity is a child of God. God offers us an invitation to accept Him as our heavenly Father. We get to make the choice if we will accept God's invitation to father us. He truly is the best Father.

GRACE – To forgive and to show love, even when people do something you may not like. They may not deserve it, but God teaches us that grace helps us love others better.

GRACIOUS – To be forgiving and caring, to do what is right. When someone wrongs us, we must be gracious and forgive, just as Jesus forgave us.

HEALING – When God makes our bodies work the way they are supposed to. When an sickness or damaged part of our body is fixed by God's supernatural restoration.

HEAVEN – God lives in our hearts and in the world around us, but heaven is a place where God also lives. There is no more sadness or any bad thing in heaven. Heaven is a perfect place.

HEAVENLY – To be of God, having godly characteristics and qualities. To care about the things God cares about and act in a way that is pleasing to Him.

HEAVENLY FATHER – God is our Father in heaven who watches over, guides, and protects us. We may not see Him like we see an earthly father, but our heavenly Father is always present. He cares about what we care about and loves it when we talk with Him.

HEAVENLY GIFT – God has given every single person on the earth one or more special gifts. God has given us many gifts, like life on earth, our family, and Jesus.

HOLY SPIRIT – The Spirit of God lives inside you and all around you. The Holy Spirit instructs you on how to make good decisions and leads you on the correct path of life.

HONOR – To have respect for someone. It is important to treat friends, parents, babysitters, and pastors with honor and respect. When you honor those around you, you honor God, too.

HOPEFUL – To be happy for the future and not afraid about any part of life because God has it all under control. God wants us to have hope and think positively about the things to come.

HUMANITY – Every person on earth who God created.

HUMILITY – To not take credit for yourself, but to remember that all good things come from Jesus.

IDENTITY – The special things about you that make you unique and different from others.

IMAGINATION – The creativity and wonder that God put inside of our heads and hearts to create amazing images and fun things. Imagination makes the world a fun place to live in. It brings life and color to the world.

INDIVIDUAL EXPRESSION – An individual's unique creations and ideas. God gave you individual expression to show the world the wonderful things that only you can do. Individual expression is a beautiful thing that we should all be thankful for and use to glorify God.

JESUS – God's only Son, sent from heaven. He lived a perfect life here on earth, and He is the best example of how to live our own lives. He loves us so much that He gave up His own life so that every person who loves Him can live with God forever in heaven.

JOHN THE BAPTIST – He was the cousin of Jesus. He spoke very highly of Jesus and told the people about Him. He was the man who baptized Jesus.

JUSTICE – Something that is done with fairness and equality. God sees and knows everything, and He will make sure everything on earth is done with justice, even if we have to wait until we get to heaven to see it.

KINDNESS – To be gentle and have a caring spirit, to love other people and care for those around you. To have a positive attitude and be willing to give of time and goods in order to help others.

KING DAVID – A king from the Old Testament who loved God and wrote many songs. King David celebrated the beauty of heaven and loved to praise God through song and dance.

KINGDOM – God's government and dominion. Jesus talked about the kingdom of God coming upon us many times, which meant that the rules and systems of government of heaven are the ones we are to live by.

LAWS – There are heavenly laws and earthly laws. Laws in our country are rules that are put together by the government to help everyone have a safe and happy life.

LEADERS – Those who are gifted in leading others in small or big ways. These people can encourage others to live for God. They can help many people when they show them the right way to live and are good examples of how God would have them act on this earth.

LIFE LESSONS AND TRIALS – Things that happen in life that seem very hard and may make you sad. Life lessons challenge you and also teach you something when you overcome them. No life lesson or trial is too hard when you have God on your side!

LOVE – A strong, positive feeling for another person or thing. God first showed us love by sending his Son, Jesus, to the world. Love is the positive way we feel towards our family and friends. Love creates good things.

MELODIES – The musical sounds that come out of an instrument or someone's singing voice. Melodies are beautiful and bring joy to people who listen to them.

MINISTER – This is someone employed by a church to share about God and His love.

MIRACLES – Amazing, good, wonderful acts or events that happen by the power of God.

OBEDIENCE – This is when you do what you are asked or told to by God, your parents, or even a teacher, even when you don't want to do it.

PASTORAL HEART – To have a heart that loves others no matter what the situation is. A pastoral heart is nurturing, loving, and protecting. People with pastoral hearts care for the broken, hungry, wounded, and needy.

PASTORS – Those who preach in a church and tell others about God and truths from the Bible. They care for those in their church and for others as a mother bird cares for her chicks. Their hearts go out to the lost and they desire to bring spiritual health to every family. The earth is a blessed place because of pastors and what they do.

PEACE – Being free from any sad or troubling thoughts or events in your life. Peace brings our happiness and freedom. Peace means to be calm and relaxed, knowing that you are safe, even if everything in your life is not perfect.

PERFECT WILL OF GOD – This is what God desires to have happen here on earth. He wants what is good and happy to happen to all humans. His plan for each and every person is perfect, and we must listen to what God has to say for our lives so that His will can be accomplished.

PERSPECTIVE – A certain way of thinking about something. When we have a heavenly perspective, we are thinking about how God wants us to act and how we can best spread God's Word throughout the world.

PRESENCE OF GOD – When God is revealing Himself by His Spirit for you to personally experience Him.

PRAYING/TO PRAY – Praying is when you talk with God. God knows what you want in your heart, but He loves it when you talk to Him in prayer. Praying can mean saying thank you to God, asking Him for help, or just telling Him about your day.

PROMISE – This is when someone assures you he or she will do something. An example of a promise is when God assures us that He will always be with us.

PROPHECY – Speaking out the heart of God when it's about something right now or future realities.

PROPHETIC VOICES – Words that speak truth and life and joy into people's lives. It's done by hearing from God and sharing His will and voice with others. A prophet is an example of someone who speaks with a prophetic voice into the lives of people.

PROPHETIC WORD – A word given from the heart of God through whatever instrument God chooses. This word will be about something right now or future realities.

PROPHETS – Those who help us to hear the heart of God. They are a gift to the body of Christ. Prophets speak words of peace and bring heaven's heart to the earth. They are amazing people because they desire to hear and speak what God has to say to us. They can see what is possible for the future and work to make it possible today.

PROSPER – To succeed in something and be successful, to further the kingdom of God. It is a very good thing and helps people to be happy.

PROTECTION – The act of being kept safe and free from harm. God's strong arms offer the best protection.

QUIET STRENGTH – This is power.

RELIABLE – When someone is trusted and can be counted on to help anyone in need.

RESTORATION – To make something beautiful, whole, and the way it was originally intended to be. People like apostles have a heart for restoration because they want God to be glorified all through the earth, which is the way it is supposed to be.

RIGHTEOUSNESS – The character trait of doing what is right and truthful in the eyes of God. Righteousness brings honor to God, and to those around you, when you display this trait with a loving heart.

SALVATION – To believe that Jesus is God's Son, that He came to earth to save us from our sins, and that He will live inside us. Salvation is the path to heaven. Jesus promises we will be with Him forever through salvation.

SELFLESS – To put someone else's needs before your own.

SERVANTS – Those who help and serve others with love and care in their hearts. They do not worry about whether or not they will receive a prize in return, but they work for the good of others.

SPIRITUALLY HUNGRY – To have a desire for God that can be relatable to your natural desires; you want to be fed and nourished by more of God.

SOLOMON – Solomon is a man of God twho built the greatest temple for God. God made Solomon the richest and wisest king to live on earth.

SON – a male child of parents.

SUMMER CAMP – a place where children gather together in the summer to do recreational activities.

SUPPORTIVE – To help another person and to provide practical and positive encouragement in the lives of those around you.

TEACHERS – Those who teach others. They help people to obtain knowledge in many areas of life; they can teach about God and show people the correct way to live. They also teach others how to love and how to hear God.

TEAMWORK – To work together with other people to accomplish a job or play a game. Teamwork is an important thing because it teaches you how to get along with others, and it makes everyone happy.

TESTIMONY – Someone's personal story. The greatest testimony is the beautiful story of God and how He sent His Son to earth to love and rescue people. Your testimony tells other people about your faith, and your story praises God through words and actions.

TO BE SAVED – To believe that Jesus Christ is God's one true Son and that He came to earth to save all humans. When we have Jesus in our hearts, God promises we will live a happy life with Him forever.

TO RESCUE – To save someone from harm's way, to let people know how much God loves them and wants them to do what He says.

TO SERVE – To put time and energy into helping others in need. It means to put someone else's needs or wants before your own. This pleases God greatly.

TO WORSHIP/WORSHIPER – To say thank you to God by singing, dancing, praying, or even writing. A worshiper loves God with all of his or her heart and wants to celebrate all of the wonderful things that He has done!

TREASURE – Something that is very precious and important to you. Something you hold very close to your heart.

TREE OF LIFE FRUIT – The fruit that Jesus gave permission to Adam and Eve to eat of in the garden of Eden.

TRUTH – That which is right and holy and true in God's eyes. Truth sets people free and gives people joy and contentment.

UNITY – To work together peacefully with someone or something. When a group of people get along with each other and agree with things, they have unity. It is important that team members have unity to peacefully complete a job.

VICTORY – To win a battle or a struggle. It helps people go far in life. It is important to give thanks to God for every victory in your life.

VISION – An image that you get in your mind about something that you want to happen that glorifies God.

VULNERABLE – People that can easily be harmed, such as those who might be too weak to protect themselves. For example, vulnerable children need to be cared for by parents, social workers, or nannies.

WHOLENESS – To be healthy and complete, free of sickness or other bad things.

WISDOM – A fruit of the Spirit or character quality that helps people to make good decisions. All wisdom comes from God. Some examples of people who have wisdom are teachers, parents, pastors, librarians, and counselors. They serve and teach others with that knowledge.

WORD OF KNOWLEDGE – A known fact that God shares with someone that is a past or present reality, like a birthdate, a phone number, or details about a certain thing that's happening. The purpose of a word of knowledge is to bring people into deeper relationship with God and impact their lives today.

WORD OF WISDOM – God gives you practical information to divinely assist someone with a word of knowledge or prophecy they have received.

WORLD CHANGER – Someone who knows who he or she is in Jesus and partners with God to make lasting change on the earth, in a job, and in the lives of people.

GROWING UP WITH GOD
Chapter Book

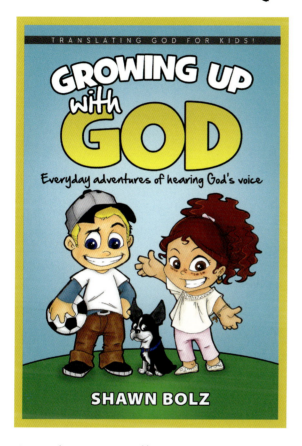

Join Lucas and Maria and friends on their everyday adventures in friendship with God!

Lucas knows God talks to him, but he would have never imagined that he would hear such a specific thing about his year . . . and could Maria really have heard God about her destiny? They both have to wonder if God speaks to kids this way. Over the months that follow, God begins to connect them to other kids that grow into friends. Who could have guessed that by the end of the year, their lives would be so exciting!

Award-winning illustrator Lamont Hunt illustrates the rich, vibrant God journey of kids you can relate to. By best-selling author Shawn Bolz.

Growing Up with God is an amazing adventure!

growingupwithgod.com

GROWING UP WITH GOD
Coloring Book

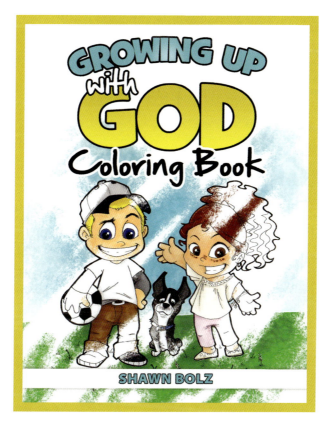

Growing Up with God has a coloring book!

In *Growing Up with God*, Lucas, Maria, and their friends spend the year on a journey of listening to God's heart of love. Through it, they learn how to support and believe in themselves and everyone around them. In this coloring book, your kids will experience the satisfaction of adding vibrant colors to the artwork of renowned character design and animation expert, Lamont Hunt. Along the way, they'll be reminded of the life lessons shared in the chapter book.

This coloring book is awaiting your child's unique passion to color these characters to life.

growingupwithgod.com

GROWING UP WITH GOD
Workbook

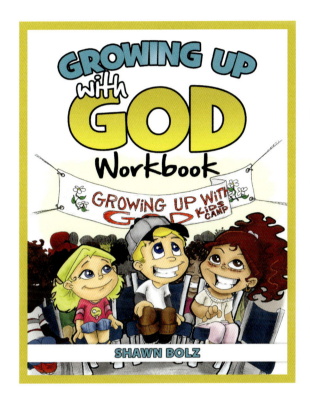

An accompaniment for *Growing Up with God*, the children's chapter book, this workbook will encourage your kids to practice hearing God's voice.

Not only does this workbook teach children how to listen to God, it also gives them the tools they need to support and believe in themselves and each other.

In each section that relates to a chapter in *Growing Up with God*, your children will find:

- A reminder of what was in the chapter
- A true story from a kid their age about how he or she encountered God
- Three important things to know about God's voice
- Bible verses to back up the teaching
- Questions for them to think about and answer
- A prayer
- Illustrations from the book to keep the content focused & exciting

This generation of kids will be the most powerful, prophetic generation yet, and this workbook is a journal and guide will help them fulfill that destiny.

growingupwithgod.com

Shawn grew up in a passionately Christian home with parents who were actively involved in his spiritual growth. Because of seeing how nurturing a relationship with God starts at a young age (Shawn and his wife, Cherie, both got saved at the age of three), he loves seeing the next generation empowered with tools that help them take their faith seriously.

Shawn is a best-selling author, conference and event speaker, TV host, and pastor in Los Angeles. Writing and telling stories are two of his favorite pastimes.

Lamont Hunt is an award-winning character animator and illustrator, currently living in the Los Angeles area. He grew up in Springfield, VA, and Memphis, TN, but most of his growing up was done in the Sioux Falls area of South Dakota. He went on to gain a BFA in drawing/illustration/graphic design at the University of Nebraska-Lincoln. Go Huskers! He gained more specialized education in animation at the Art Institute International, MN, Animation Mentor, and Animsquad. Lamont has worked as an artist/illustrator and animator in South Dakota, Minnesota, Taiwan, and California, and with companies like The Jim Henson Co. and Ken Duncan Studio. *Growing Up with God* is his first illustrated children's book.

TEACHERS REPRODUCIBLE PAGES

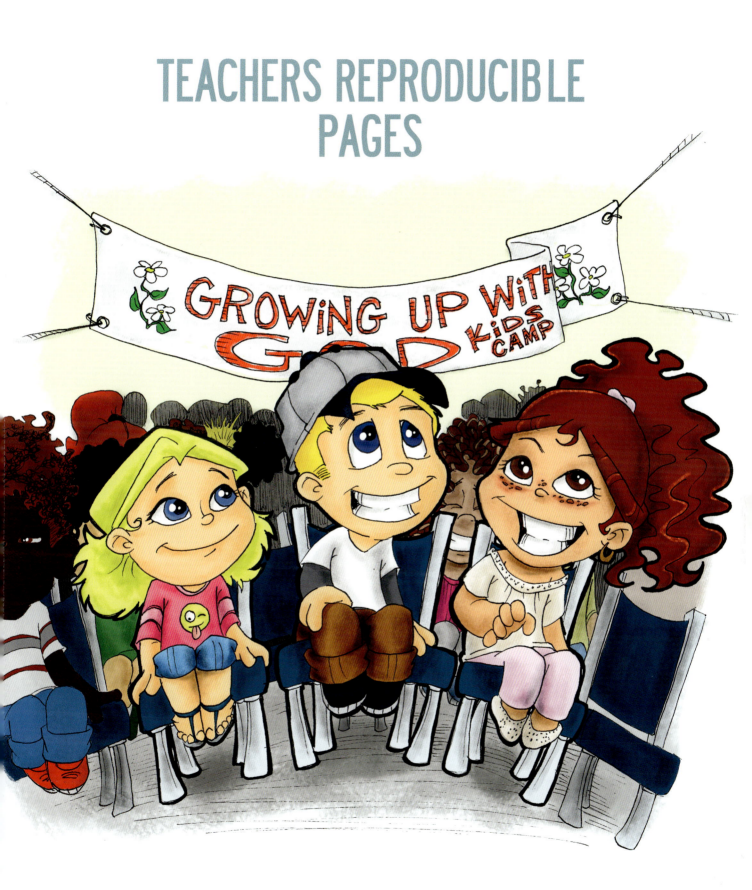

CHAPTER 1 CHECKLIST

- ☐ Read Chapter 1 in *Growing Up with God*
- ☐ Choose DVD – Option One or Two
- ☐ Read aloud: Student testimonials
- ☐ Review with Students: Synopsis

TEACHING POINT 1:
CONNECTING WITH GOD AS A FRIEND

- ☐ Teach / Review Biblical Foundations
  Biblical Foundations 1.1:
  "Believing Births Friendship"
- ☐ Share: Student Key Verse
  John 10:10
- ☐ Teach / Review: Teaching Content 1
  Connecting with God as a Friend
- ☐ Student Question / Reflection
  When was the first time you felt like God was your friend? What did you feel? Maybe you didn't feel anything but you just knew. How did you know?

TEACHING POINT 2:
HOW FRIENDSHIP WITH GOD IS INTERACTIVE

- ☐ Teach / Review Biblical Foundations
  Biblical Foundations 1.2:
  "God Covers Us with Friendship"
- ☐ Share: Student Key Verse
  John 16:7
- ☐ Teach / Review: Teaching Content 2
  How Friendship is Interactive
- ☐ Student Question / Reflection
  The Holy Spirit was Jesus's friend, and they had a lot of fun and good conversations together. Jesus said the Holy Spirit takes from God and delivers it to you. What do you think of that?

TEACHING POINT 3:
LEARN HOW TO LISTEN

- ☐ Teach / Review Biblical Foundation
  Biblical Foundations 1.3:
  "Practice Listening"
- ☐ Share: Student Key Verse
  John 10:3
- ☐ Teach / Review: Teaching Content 3
  Learning How to Listen
- ☐ Student Question / Reflection
  Maria was worried that she might never be able to hear God talk to her. Have you ever worried about that too, and have you talked to God about it? He can always hear you. Write down anything you're nervous about when you think about hearing God talk to you.

PRAY GROWTH PRAYER

GROWTH ACTIVITIES

- ☐ Individual
- ☐ Group
- ☐ Activity Page
- ☐ Coloring Page
- ☐ Implement parenting tip into weekly life

WHAT ATTRIBUTES ARE IMPORTANT TO ME IN FRIENDSHIP?

Write down the qualities you would want a friend of yours to have. For example: loyalty, confidentiality, bravery, fun to be around, musical talent, spiritual strength, cleverness, athleticism, relational skills, leadership qualities, celebratory personality, truthfulness, kindness, sensitivity, or helpfulness.

Scripture: "When the Friend comes, the Spirit of the Truth, he will take you by the hand and guide you into all the truth there is."
– John 16:12

CHAPTER 2 CHECKLIST

- ☐ Read Chapter 2 in *Growing Up with God*
- ☐ Choose DVD – Option One or Two
- ☐ Read aloud: Student testimonials
- ☐ Review with Students: Synopsis

TEACHING POINT 4:
GO ON A GOD JOURNEY WITH YOUR CLOSE FRIENDS AND FAMILY

- ☐ Teach / Review Biblical Foundations
  Biblical Foundations 2.1:
  "Jesus Starts the Best Journeys"
- ☐ Share: Student Key Verse
  Hebrews 10:23
- ☐ Teach / Review: Teaching Content 4
  Go on a God journey
- ☐ Student Question / Reflection

  Have you ever shared some things God tells you with friends and your family? How did they react?

  Lucas's mom was excited to hear Lucas talk about his word from God. She encouraged him and told him he was special. How can you encourage and help others to get more connected to God?

TEACHING POINT 5:
TREASURE WHAT GOD TELLS YOU

- ☐ Teach / Review Biblical Foundations
  Biblical Foundations 2.2:
  "God's Kingdom Is Like a Treasure"
- ☐ Share: Student Key Verse
  Luke 2:19
- ☐ Teach / Review: Teaching Content 5
  Treasure what God tells you
- ☐ Student Question / Reflection

TEACHING POINT 5: CONTINUED...
TREASURE WHAT GOD TELLS YOU

Do you treasure the things God has told you? Do you think about them when you are making decisions about your life? It's important to do! What are some things you could do to help you remember?

TEACHING POINT 6:
HELP OTHERS HAVE FAITH TO CONNECT TO GOD

- ☐ Teach / Review Biblical Foundations
  Biblical Foundations 2.3:
  "Be Jesus to the World"
- ☐ Share: Student Key Verse
  Hebrews 10:24
- ☐ Teach / Review: Teaching Content 6
  Help others have faith to connect to God
- ☐ Student Question / Reflection

  God made you to be creative about coming up with ways to connect with His heart. If you stop and think about that right now, what are some things you could start doing to connect to Him more?

PRAY GROWTH PRAYER

GROWTH ACTIVITIES

- ☐ Individual
- ☐ Group
- ☐ Activity Page
- ☐ Coloring Page
- ☐ Implement parenting tip into weekly life

MY SPIRITUAL MAP MOMENTS

Write down five memories you have of moments in your life that were really important to you and God. One could be of the time when you got saved, or when you first learned how to pray. It could be a time when God spoke something to you. On the "X marks the spot" place on the map, write in the most significant of your God journey moments.

Scripture: But Mary treasured up all these things and pondered them in her heart. — Luke 2:19

CHAPTER 3 CHECKLIST

- ☐ Read Chapter 3 in *Growing Up with God*
- ☐ Choose DVD – Option One or Two
- ☐ Read aloud: Student testimonials
- ☐ Review with Students: Synopsis

TEACHING POINT 7:
GOD HAS A BIGGER PICTURE IN MIND WHEN HE TELLS YOU THINGS

- ☐ Teach / Review Biblical Foundations
  Biblical Foundations 3.1:
  "Master Plans From God"
- ☐ Share: Student Key Verse
  Ephesians 3:20
- ☐ Teach / Review: Teaching Content 7
  God has a bigger picture
- ☐ Student Question / Reflection
  When God gives you a word or tells you something about the future, why do you think He usually make those things happen in ways you don't expect?

TEACHING POINT 8:
YOUR PROCESS IS SOMETIMES DIFFERENT EVERYONE ELSE'S

- ☐ Teach / Review Biblical Foundations
  Biblical Foundations 3.2:
  "Be Who You Are"
- ☐ Share: Student Key Verse
  Galatians 6:4-5
- ☐ Teach / Review: Teaching Content 8
  Your process is sometimes different to everyone else's
- ☐ Student Question / Reflection
  What kind of spiritual upgrades has God already given you? What has He done in your life and in your heart that has made you feel more connected to Him?

TEACHING POINT 9:
SEEING GOD MAKE THINGS HAPPEN FOR SOMEONE ELSE

- ☐ Teach / Review Biblical Foundations
  Biblical Foundations 3.3:
  "God Will Do The Same for You"
- ☐ Share: Student Key Verse
  John 14:12
- ☐ Teach / Review: Teaching Content 9
  Seeing God make things happen for someone else
- ☐ Student Question / Reflection
  What examples have you seen in your own life and in your friends' lives to prove that God wants to bless everyone with a close connection to His heart?

PRAY GROWTH PRAYER

GROWTH ACTIVITIES

- ☐ Individual
- ☐ Group
- ☐ Activity Page
- ☐ Coloring Page
- ☐ Implement parenting tip into weekly life

GOD WANTS TO SPEAK TO ME!

Try some listening prayer. In the first box, write down something you think you hear God saying to you. In the second box, write down the name of a friend, parent, or family member. Ask God to tell you something about that person. Write what He says into that box, too.

Scripture: Anyone who looks will see, anyone who listens will hear.
– Isaiah 32:1–8

CHAPTER 4 CHECKLIST

- ☐ Read Chapter 4 in *Growing Up with God*
- ☐ Choose DVD – Option One or Two
- ☐ Read aloud: Student testimonials
- ☐ Review with Students: Synopsis

TEACHING POINT 10:
RECOGNIZE THE PRESENCE OF GOD AND TAKE CHANCES

- ☐ Teach / Review Biblical Foundations
  Biblical Foundations 4.1:
  "Promises Aren't Always Free"
- ☐ Share: Student Key Verse
  Matthew 5:14
- ☐ Teach / Review: Teaching Content 10
  Recognize the presence of God and take chances
- ☐ Student Question / Reflection
  Is there anything you are afraid might happen if you are brave and do what God asks you to do? What would make you less afraid?

TEACHING POINT 11:
TAKE SMALL STEPS OF RISK TO START GROWING

- ☐ Teach / Review Biblical Foundations
  Biblical Foundations 4.2:
  "Grow by Steps"
- ☐ Share: Student Key Verse
  James 1:16
- ☐ Teach / Review: Teaching Content 11
  Take small steps of risk to start growing
- ☐ Student Question / Reflection
  What small steps can you take this week that will help you grow in love? If you have already done some kind acts, what difference have you seen them make in the lives of those around you?

TEACHING POINT 12:
BE ON THE LOOKOUT FOR WAYS TO APPLY WORDS TO CURRENT CIRCUMSTANCES

- ☐ Teach / Review Biblical Foundations
  Biblical Foundations 4.3:
  "Waiting on Him"
- ☐ Share: Student Key Verse
  Colossians 3:12-14
- ☐ Teach / Review: Teaching Content 12
  Be on the lookout for ways to apply words to current circumstances
- ☐ Student Question / Reflection
  When you look at your Christian friends' lives, when do you see them acting like Jesus? How do you think they grow into being more like Him?

PRAY GROWTH PRAYER

GROWTH ACTIVITIES

- ☐ Individual
- ☐ Group
- ☐ Activity Page
- ☐ Coloring Page
- ☐ Implement parenting tip into weekly life

MY CALLING AND THE STEPS TO GET THERE

In the box at the bottom of Jamal's ladder, write down one or more of the things you are called to. Examples: "I am called to act." "I am called to preach." "I am called to be a policeman." "I am called to worship." "I am called to teach."

1. On the first rung of the ladder, write something you know you'll need to do to fulfill your calling (like a specific training class you can go to).

2. On the second ladder rung, write down a step you have seen someone else take toward the same calling—because learning from others' lives helps us to pursue our own calling.

3. On the third rung, ask God to show you one step you can take now toward fulfilling your calling. Keep asking for steps and see how many he will give you up the ladder!

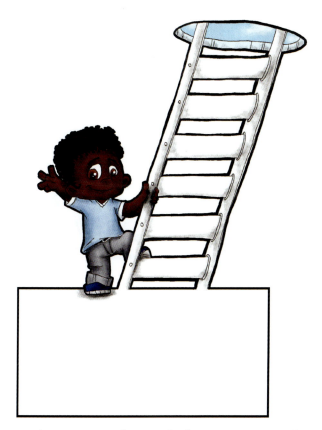

Scripture: Strength! Courage! Don't be timid; don't get discouraged. God, your God, is with you every step you take. – Joshua 1:9

CHAPTER 5 CHECKLIST

☐ Read Chapter 5 in *Growing Up with God*
☐ Choose DVD – Option One or Two
☐ Read aloud: Student testimonials
☐ Review with Students: Synopsis

TEACHING POINT 13:
SOMETIMES GOD LEADS YOU TO YOUR GOALS IN INDIRECT WAYS

☐ Teach / Review Biblical Foundations
Biblical Foundations 5.1:
"God Is Our Guide"

☐ Share: Student Key Verse
1 Corinthians 13:2

☐ Teach / Review: Teaching Content 13
Sometimes God leads you to your goals in indirect ways

☐ Student Question / Reflection
How does it feel different in your heart when you do things for your parents out of obedience compared to when you do things for them out of love? Which way makes you feel more connected?

TEACHING POINT 14:
SOMETIMES LIFE HAS OBSTACLES IN THE WAY OF YOUR PROMISES

☐ Teach / Review Biblical Foundations
Biblical Foundations 5.2:
"Never Give Up"

☐ Share: Student Key Verse
James 1:2

☐ Teach / Review: Teaching Content 14
Sometimes life has obstacles in the way of your promises

☐ Student Question / Reflection
Was there ever a time when it looked like God wasn't doing what He'd promised, but then it turned out He was making it happen all along?

TEACHING POINT 15:
YOU ARE ALWAYS CALLED TO THE WHO, NOT THE WHAT

☐ Teach / Review Biblical Foundations
Biblical Foundations 5.3:
"People Are Our Destiny"

☐ Share: Student Key Verse
1 John 3:18

☐ Teach / Review: Teaching Content 15
You are always called to the who, not the what

☐ Student Question / Reflection
If you did nothing the right way ever again, would God still love you and want to bless you? (See Ephesians 2:8-10) That's the kind of love He wants to give you for other people.

PRAY GROWTH PRAYER

GROWTH ACTIVITIES

☐ Individual
☐ Group
☐ Activity Page
☐ Coloring Page
☐ Implement parenting tip into weekly life

WHO IS MY DESTINY!

Who are you called to love? God never puts His light at the bottom of a hill but on the highest place it can shine from! Inside the mountain, write down all the types of people you are called to love to fulfill your destiny. This is where you get to rule in love. For example, if you are called to be a nurse, then you are called to love patients, doctors, other nurses, emergency workers, etc.

Scripture: Live out your God-created identity. Live generously and graciously toward others, the way God lives toward you. – Matthew 5:48

CHAPTER 6 CHECKLIST

- ☐ Read Chapter 6 in *Growing Up with God*
- ☐ Choose DVD – Option One or Two
- ☐ Read aloud: Student testimonials
- ☐ Review with Students: Synopsis

TEACHING POINT 16:
LISTEN TO GOD, EVEN WHEN WHAT HE TELLS YOU TO DO IS HARD

- ☐ Teach / Review Biblical Foundations
  Biblical Foundations 6.1:
  "Recognizing His Voice Builds Friendship"
- ☐ Share: Student Key Verse
  Proverbs 3:6
- ☐ Teach / Review: Teaching Content 16
  Listen to God
- ☐ Student Question / Reflection
  What do you think Matthew 7:13-14 means, to "enter through the narrow gate?" The narrow gate "leads to life, and only a few find it." Why do you think it's so important to Jesus that we do things His way?

TEACHING POINT 17:
TREASURE WHAT GOD TELLS YOU

- ☐ Teach / Review Biblical Foundations
  Biblical Foundations 6.2:
  "You Can Recognize His Voice"
- ☐ Share: Student Key Verse
  John 16:29-30
- ☐ Teach / Review: Teaching Content 17
  Treasure what God tells you
- ☐ Student Question / Reflection
  Sometimes we can get tired waiting for God to do what He's promised. What can you do to keep trusting Him and doing what He wants you to do?

TEACHING POINT 18:
GOD IS ALWAYS TEACHING YOU AND SHARING HIMSELF WITH YOU

- ☐ Teach / Review Biblical Foundations
  Biblical Foundations 6.3:
  "God Is Our Teacher"
- ☐ Share: Student Key Verse
  1 Timothy 4:12
- ☐ Teach / Review: Teaching Content 18
  God is always teaching you and sharing Himself with you
- ☐ Student Question / Reflection
  What are some ways you could spend more time with God and grow your friendship with Him?

PRAY GROWTH PRAYER

GROWTH ACTIVITIES

- ☐ Individual
- ☐ Group
- ☐ Activity Page
- ☐ Coloring Page
- ☐ Implement parenting tip into weekly life

I WILL SEE PEOPLE AS IF THEY'VE ALREADY WON AT LIFE

On the trophy, write the names of three people that you are called to see in fullness at the end of their lives, as if they have already won the trophy for living out their purpose well. Tell God you are willing to see them this way, and then write something you see about them that maybe they haven't accomplished yet, but that you will believe for. For example: "She will go to college to get a master's degree." "He will make a lot of money in business." "He will be a great athlete."

Scripture: With both feet planted firmly on love, you'll be able to take in with all followers of Jesus the extravagant dimensions of Christ's love. Reach out and experience the breadth! Test its length! Plumb the depths! Rise to the heights! Live full lives, full in the fullness of God.
– Ephesians 3:14-19

CHAPTER 7 CHECKLIST

- ☐ Read Chapter 7 in *Growing Up with God*
- ☐ Choose DVD – Option One or Two
- ☐ Read aloud: Student testimonials
- ☐ Review with Students: Synopsis

TEACHING POINT 19:
YOUR GOAL IS TO LOVE

- ☐ Teach / Review Biblical Foundations
  Biblical Foundations 7.1:
  "Love Is The Only Way"
- ☐ Share: Student Key Verse
  Philippians 2:2
- ☐ Teach / Review: Teaching Content 19
  Your goal is to love
- ☐ Student Question / Reflection
  Have you ever stopped doing something for yourself and focused on helping someone else instead? How did that feel?

TEACHING POINT 20:
TAKE RISKS WITH WHAT YOU HEAR FROM GOD

- ☐ Teach / Review Biblical Foundations
  Biblical Foundations 7.2:
  "Taking Risk Is Important"
- ☐ Share: Student Key Verse
  Hebrews 4:12
- ☐ Teach / Review: Teaching Content 20
  Take risks with what you hear from God
- ☐ Student Question / Reflection
  Have you ever obeyed what you thought Jesus was saying to do even though it was hard? What happened?

TEACHING POINT 21:
WHEN YOU OBEY GOD AND WALK WITH HIM, YOU CAN'T HELP BUT FEEL HIS FRIENDSHIP

- ☐ Teach / Review Biblical Foundations
  Biblical Foundations 7.3:
  "Trust Brings Adventure"
- ☐ Share: Student Key Verse
  Ephesians 1:17
- ☐ Teach / Review: Teaching Content 21
  When you obey God and walk with Him, you can't help but feel His friendship
- ☐ Student Question / Reflection
  How has God done good things in your heart and life after hard times or pain?

PRAY GROWTH PRAYER

GROWTH ACTIVITIES

- ☐ Individual
- ☐ Group
- ☐ Activity Page
- ☐ Coloring Page
- ☐ Implement parenting tip into weekly life

I WILL TAKE SPIRITUAL RISKS!

It is worth taking a risk as a Christian to do something you think God has asked you to do. The worst that could happen is that nothing gets better, or your friends make fun of you. Under Jesus's foot/in the water, draw or write something that would be a big spiritual risk for you to take. Now pray God gives you the opportunity to take it!

Scripture: I ask—ask the God of our Master, Jesus Christ, the God of glory—to make you intelligent and discerning in knowing him personally, your eyes focused and clear, so that you can see exactly what it is he is calling you to do, grasp the immensity of this glorious way of life he has for his followers. — Ephesians 1:17-18

CHAPTER 8 CHECKLIST

- ☐ Read Chapter 8 in *Growing Up with God*
- ☐ Choose DVD – Option One or Two
- ☐ Read aloud: Student testimonials
- ☐ Review with Students: Synopsis

TEACHING POINT 22:
YOUR FRIENDSHIP WITH GOD EVEN HELPS THOSE WHO DON'T KNOW HIM!

- ☐ Teach / Review Biblical Foundations
  Biblical Foundations 8.1:
  "Your Relationship Changes Everything"
- ☐ Share: Student Key Verse
  Galatians 6:4
- ☐ Teach / Review: Teaching Content 22
  Your friendship with God even helps those who don't know Him
- ☐ Student Question / Reflection
  How has God's love from other people helped your heart? Can you imagine how other people's hearts could fill up on His love when you love them like Jesus, even if they don't know Him?

TEACHING POINT 23:
YOU CAN BLESS OTHERS BY GIVING AWAY WHAT GOD HAS GIVEN YOU

- ☐ Teach / Review Biblical Foundations
  Biblical Foundations 8.2:
  "Generosity Is Contagious"
- ☐ Share: Student Key Verse
  Matthew 18:20
- ☐ Teach / Review: Teaching Content 23
  You can bless others by giving away what God has given you
- ☐ Student Question / Reflection
  If you think about the ideas and thoughts you've already come up with in your times with God, which ones do you know were ideas

TEACHING POINT 23: CONTINUED...
YOU CAN BLESS OTHERS BY GIVING AWAY WHAT GOD HAS GIVEN YOU

and thoughts given to you by God? Can you see how God could use some of them to help make other people's lives better?

TEACHING POINT 24:
GOD BRINGS SOMETHING GOOD OUT OF EVERYTHING

- ☐ Teach / Review Biblical Foundations
  Biblical Foundations 8.3:
  "God Is Good"
- ☐ Share: Student Key Verse
  Romans 8:28
- ☐ Teach / Review: Teaching Content 24
  God brings something good out of everything
- ☐ Student Question / Reflection
  Can you see where God has brought something good out of some of the sad things that have happened in your life?

PRAY GROWTH PRAYER

GROWTH ACTIVITIES

- ☐ Individual
- ☐ Group
- ☐ Activity Page
- ☐ Coloring Page
- ☐ Implement parenting tip into weekly life

I AM CALLED TO HAVE FAVOR
AND TO INFLUENCE THOSE AROUND ME, LIKE JOSEPH!

Joseph's father gave him an extravagant coat that had many colors. In the Spirit you wear many virtues—parts of God's character—just like Joseph wore that coat. Color the virtues that are the ones you feel you will operate in and influence people with.

Scripture: He knows us far better than we know ourselves . . . and keeps us present before God. That's why we can be so sure that every detail in our lives of love for God is worked into something good. — Romans 8:26–28

CHAPTER 9 CHECKLIST

☐ Read Chapter 9 in *Growing Up with God*
☐ Choose DVD – Option One or Two
☐ Read aloud: Student testimonials
☐ Review with Students: Synopsis

TEACHING POINT 25:
GOD SPEAKS OUT OF RELATIONSHIP AND GROWS YOUR FRIENDSHIP WITH HIM

☐ Teach / Review Biblical Foundations
Biblical Foundations 9.1:
"Relationship Bring Revelation"

☐ Share: Student Key Verse
Luke 12:4

☐ Teach / Review: Teaching Content 25
God speaks out of relationship and grows your friendship with Him

☐ Student Question / Reflection
If you were going to give yourself a score out of ten, how much would you say you know Jesus right now? What could you do to know Him more?

TEACHING POINT 26:
WHEN GOD ISN'T SPEAKING, IT IS BECAUSE HE WANTS YOU TO GROW IN YOUR IDENTITY

☐ Teach / Review Biblical Foundations
Biblical Foundations 9.2:
"God Loves to Give Us Choice"

☐ Share: Student Key Verse
Galatians 5:16

☐ Teach / Review: Teaching Content 26
When God isn't speaking, it is because He wants you to grow in your identity

☐ Student Question / Reflection
Jesus wants you to know yourself—what you like, how you like it, what your character strengths are, what your personality is like, and how you do things. Why do you think He cares so much about helping you be you?

TEACHING POINT 27:
WHEN YOU ACT LIKE JESUS WITH YOUR FRIENDS, THERE IS ALWAYS A BENEFIT

☐ Teach / Review Biblical Foundations
Biblical Foundations 9.3:
"Becoming Like Jesus"

☐ Share: Student Key Verse
Hebrews 10:24

☐ Teach / Review: Teaching Content 27
When you act like Jesus with your friends, there is always a benefit

☐ Student Question / Reflection
Some kids find that the more they know God, the easier it is to make choices that benefit not just themselves, but the people around them too. Would you agree? Why/why not…

PRAY GROWTH PRAYER

GROWTH ACTIVITIES

☐ Individual
☐ Group
☐ Activity Page
☐ Coloring Page
☐ Implement parenting tip into weekly life

THE HOLY SPIRIT IS NOT
A JUNIOR IN ME, BUT A FULL HOLY SPIRIT!

God is not limited to our size or maturity. Write words that describe what you can grow in—God will help you practice listening to the Holy Spirit and growing in love. For example: "I can prophesy." "I can heal the sick." "I can listen." "I can pray for people." "I can intercede." "I can create." "I can love." "I can share my faith."

Scripture: So let's do it—full of belief, confident that we're presentable inside and out. Let's keep a firm grip on the promises that keep us going. He always keeps his word. Let's see how inventive we can be in encouraging love and helping out . . . spurring each other on.
— Hebrews 10:22-24

CHAPTER 10 CHECKLIST

- ☐ Read Chapter 10 in *Growing Up with God*
- ☐ Choose DVD – Option One or Two
- ☐ Read aloud: Student testimonials
- ☐ Review with Students: Synopsis

TEACHING POINT 28:
YOU CAN LOVE WELL

- ☐ Teach / Review Biblical Foundations
  Biblical Foundations 10.1:
  "Loving Well Is a Choice"
- ☐ Share: Student Key Verse
  John 3:16-17
- ☐ Teach / Review: Teaching Content 28
  You can love well
- ☐ Student Question / Reflection
  When you think of people who show you God's love, how do they show it? Is it through preaching or through treating you in a certain way?

TEACHING POINT 29:
THE NUMBER-ONE WAY PEOPLE BECOME CHRISTIANS IS THROUGH RELATIONSHIP

- ☐ Teach / Review Biblical Foundations
  Biblical Foundations 10.2:
  "Healthy Relationship Is Important"
- ☐ Share: Student Key Verse
  1 John 4:19
- ☐ Teach / Review: Teaching Content 29
  The number one way people become christians is through relationship
- ☐ Student Question / Reflection
  What do you think is the main thing your family and friends need from you? How much of it do you need Jesus's help with?

TEACHING POINT 30:
YOU GROW IN GOD EVERY DAY

- ☐ Teach / Review Biblical Foundations
  Biblical Foundations 10.3:
  "Daily Walk with God"
- ☐ Share: Student Key Verse
  Galatians 5:22-23
- ☐ Teach / Review: Teaching Content 30
  You grow in God every day
- ☐ Student Question / Reflection
  How long do you think it takes to grow up in God so much that you end up being just like Jesus? God grows some things quickly and other things slowly. How do you know if you are growing up in God already? Do you know He loves you just as much now as He will when you have grown up in Him? That's how amazing His love is.

PRAY GROWTH PRAYER

GROWTH ACTIVITIES

- ☐ Individual
- ☐ Group
- ☐ Activity Page
- ☐ Coloring Page
- ☐ Implement parenting tip into weekly life

I CAN GROW IN CLOSENESS TO GOD!

Draw yourself into the picture, and with it, show how close you feel to Jesus. For example: Are you holding hands, are you standing close, are you far off? Don't worry if you aren't close yet; relationship takes time! If you are close, you can get even closer! In *Growing Up with God*, the friends share how much closer they have gotten since the class started. Write words beside the picture you drew of yourself that describe your closeness to Jesus.

Scripture: We, though, are going to love—love and be loved. First we were loved, now we love. He loved us first. — 1 John 4: 17–19